Windows® Phone 7

DUDLEY PUBLIC LIBRARIES

The loan of this book may be renewed if not required by other readers, by contacting the library from which it was borrowed.

Windows® Phone 7
FOR
DUMMIES®

by Bill Hughes

WILEY

Wiley Publishing, Inc.

Windows® Phone 7 For Dummies®

Published by
Wiley Publishing, Inc.
111 River Street
Hoboken, NJ 07030-5774

www.wiley.com

Copyright © 2011 by Wiley Publishing, Inc., Indianapolis, Indiana

Published simultaneously in Canada

WILEY

About the Author

Bill Hughes is an experienced marketing strategy executive with over two decades of experience in sales, strategic marketing, and business development roles at several leading corporations, including Microsoft, IBM, General Electric, Motorola, and US West Cellular.

Recently, Bill has worked with Microsoft to enhance its marketing to mobile applications developers. He also has led initiatives to develop new products and solutions with several high-tech organizations, including Nextel, Motorola, SBC, and Tyco Electronics.

Bill has been a professor of marketing at the Kellogg School of Management at Northwestern University where he taught business marketing to graduate MBA students. In his lectures, he presented his findings on the validity of the market-research information used in financial analysis.

Bill also has written articles on this subject for several wireless industry trade magazines, as well as contributed to articles in *USA Today* and *Forbes*. These articles were based upon his research reports written for In-Stat, where he was a principal analyst, covering the wireless industry, specializing in smartphones and business applications of wireless devices. His most popular studies include: "The Symbian Foundation: A Battle Royal for the Ecosystem," "Wireless Data in the Enterprise: The Hockey Stick Arrives," and "Cellphone Trends in U.S. Enterprises: A Small Step from Personal Wireless."

He graduated with honors with an MBA degree from the Kellogg School of Management at Northwestern University and earned a bachelor of science degree with distinction from the College of Engineering at Cornell University, where he was elected to the Tau Beta Pi Engineering Honorary.

Bill lives in Bellevue, Washington, with his wife, Susan, and three sons, Ellis, Arlen, and Quinlan.

Dedication

I would like to dedicate this book to my late father, Robert J. Hughes, Sr.

Author's Acknowledgments

I need to thank a number of people who helped make this book a reality. First, I would thank my literary agent, Carole Jelen, of Waterside Publishing, for her support, encouragement, knowledge, and negotiation skills.

I would also like to thank the team at Wiley Publishing: Katie Mohr, Pat O'Brien, Dan Francis, and Elizabeth Kuball. Your expertise helped me through the creative process. Thanks for your guidance.

I need to give thanks to Andrew McKenna, a student at the University of Washington who has acted as my advisor on important details of using the Xbox and Xbox LIVE. As a 40-something who has been in the wireless industry for 20 years, I could write confidently on every subject except for gaming on the Xbox, and Andrew filled me in on what I've been missing. He took time out of his summer schedule to advise me. Although his parents, Kathy and Mike, probably wanted him to spend less time playing games, I'm glad he frittered away at least some of his youth on such pursuits.

I would like to acknowledge my sons, Ellis, Arlen, and Quinlan, for keeping it quiet (other than dropping the occasional lacrosse ball on their floor/my ceiling) as I wrote this book. You can now turn up your Zune players.

Finally, and above all else, I need to acknowledge the support of my wife, Susan, who seemed to have a never-ending reservoir of patience with me as I worked to write an amusing and useful book. I'm sure the readers will appreciate her brutal honesty on what was not amusing. Although this subject matter is fascinating to me, I recognize that this was not as interesting to Susan as what was happening on *The Bachelorette*. Thanks for helping me anyway.

Publisher's Acknowledgments

We're proud of this book; please send us your comments at http://dummies.custhelp.com. For other comments, please contact our Customer Care Department within the U.S. at 877-762-2974, outside the U.S. at 317-572-3993, or fax 317-572-4002.

Some of the people who helped bring this book to market include the following:

Acquisitions and Editorial

Project Editor: Elizabeth Kuball

Sr. Acquisitions Editor: Katie Mohr

Copy Editor: Elizabeth Kuball

Technical Editor: Daniel Francis

Editorial Manager: Jodi Jensen

Editorial Assistant: Amanda Graham

Sr. Editorial Assistant: Cherie Case

Cartoons: Rich Tennant
   (www.the5thwave.com)

Composition Services

Project Coordinator: Sheree Montgomery

Layout and Graphics: Joyce Haughey,
   Lavonne Roberts

Proofreaders: John Greenough, Linda Seifert

Indexer: Ty Koontz

Publishing and Editorial for Technology Dummies

   Richard Swadley, Vice President and Executive Group Publisher

   Andy Cummings, Vice President and Publisher

   Mary Bednarek, Executive Acquisitions Director

   Mary C. Corder, Editorial Director

Publishing for Consumer Dummies

   Diane Graves Steele, Vice President and Publisher

Composition Services

   Debbie Stailey, Director of Composition Services

Contents at a Glance

Table of Contents

Introduction

*W*indows Phone 7 is a revolutionary cellular operating system that sets a new standard for convenience and productivity. It can integrate with your personal and work computers more than any other phone currently on the market. Plus, it runs a great variety of mobile applications and is great with games, music, and video.

Smartphones are getting smarter all the time, and the Windows Phone is one of the smartest. Just because you've used a smartphone in the past doesn't mean you should expect to use your new Windows Phone without a bit of guidance. That's where this book comes in. This book is a hands-on guide to getting the most out of your Windows Phone, without all the jargon that user's manuals show off with.

About This Book

This book is a reference — you don't have to read it from beginning to end to get all you need out of it. The information is clearly organized and easy to access. You don't need thick glasses and a pocket protector to understand this book.

In fact, this book is even more valuable than your user's manual. A user's manual tells how to do things, but this book helps you figure out what you want to do — and then tells you how to do it, in plain English.

Conventions Used in This Book

I don't use many conventions in this book, but there are a few you should know about:

- Whenever I introduce a new term, I put it in *italics* and define it shortly thereafter (often in parentheses).

- I use **bold** for the action parts of numbered steps, so you can easily see what you're supposed to do.

- I use `monofont` for Web addresses and e-mail addresses, so they stand out from the surrounding text. ***Note:*** When this book was printed, some Web addresses may have needed to break across two lines of text. If that happened, rest assured that we haven't put in any extra characters (such as hyphens) to indicate the break. So, when using one of these Web addresses, just type in exactly what you see in this book, pretending as though the line break doesn't exist.

Finally, some screen layouts on your PC and Windows Phone will look subtly different from what you see in this book. Sometimes this is because of differences in resolution among PCs. In the case of Windows Phone 7, Microsoft often makes creative enhancements, like changing icons. These differences should be slight and shouldn't affect your ability to understand the text.

What You're Not to Read

I think you'll find every last word of this book scintillating, but I may be a little biased. The truth is, you don't have to read

- **Sidebars:** Sidebars are those gray boxes throughout the book. They're interesting, but not essential to the topic at hand, so if you're short on time or you only want the information you absolutely need, you can skip them.

- **Text marked with the Technical Stuff icon:** For more on this icon, see the "Icons Used in This Book" section, later in this Introduction.

Foolish Assumptions

You know what they say about assuming, so I don't do much of it in this book. But I do make a few assumptions about you:

- **You have a Windows Phone.** You may be thinking about buying a Windows Phone, but my money's on your already owning one. After all, getting your hands on the phone is the best part!

- **You're not totally new to cellphones.** You know that your Windows Phone is capable of doing more than the average cellphone, and you're eager to find out what your Windows Phone can do.

- **You've used a computer.** You don't have to be a computer expert, but you at least know how to check your e-mail and surf the Web.

How This Book Is Organized

The chapters in this book are divided into eight parts. Here's what you can find in each part.

Part 1: Getting Started

The first part of this book gets you familiar with the basic capabilities of your Windows Phone. Chapter 1 is an introduction to everything from turning it on and off, to understanding cellular billing, to managing battery life. In Chapters 2 and 3, I cover the basics: placing and taking calls and sending texts.

Part II: Moving Beyond the Basics

In this part, I walk you through the full capabilities of the Windows Phone so you can decide what you want to do and what you want to ignore. Then I introduce you to the applications that come on your phone.

Part III: Live on the Internet: Going Mobile

This part is all about the Internet — how to access it from your Windows Phone and what a Windows Live ID can do for you. I also introduce you to the Windows Phone Marketplace, where you can trick out your phone with more apps.

Part IV: Connecting with the People You Care About

On your phone, you can view updates from your friends on a social networking site, as you do now on your PC. Your Windows Phone also allows you to view the updates from a given friend from all the social-networking sites that you share. Your Windows Phone brings all these updates for your friend into one page, so that you can get all the updates for that friend in one place.

This adds a new level of convenience for staying in touch with friends while you're on the go. The integration of social-networking sites is in addition to the integration and mobilizing of e-mail accounts and instant messaging services. The power of this platform is to bring together multiple messaging options for the people that are most important.

Part V: Music and Videos in the Palm of Your Hand

In this part, I cover the multimedia capabilities of the Windows Phone. Windows Phone 7 has the best capabilities of the Zune HD, a wonderfully powerful MP3 and video player. This part covers how to use your phone to listen to music and watch videos — and how to buy more music and videos from the Zune Marketplace.

Part VI: Gaming on Your Phone with Xbox LIVE

In this part, I cover gaming, one of the ways that Windows Phone 7 devices stand out from the crowd. In addition to games that you can play on the phone, Windows Phone 7 provides you with a way to play your favorite games from your Xbox! I'm talking multi-player turn games, like chess, as well as many games that are available on Xbox LIVE . . . *from your phone.* Enough said.

Part VII: Taking Care of Business with Your Windows Phone

In this part, I look at the many ways you can use your phone for business. You can bring up Microsoft Office files on Windows Phone 7. Plus, there's integration with Microsoft SharePoint, the business collaboration tool from Microsoft.

Part VIII: The Part of Tens

This wouldn't be a *For Dummies* book without a Part of Tens. In this book, the Part of Tens covers ten ways to customize the phone to make it truly your own and ten capabilities to look for in future releases.

Icons Used in This Book

Throughout this book, I use *icons* (little pictures in the margin) to draw your attention to various types of information. Here's a key to what those icons mean:

This whole book is one whole series of tips. But when I share especially useful tips and tricks, I mark it with the Tip icon.

This book is a reference, which means you don't have to commit it to memory — there is no test at the end. But once in a while, I do tell you things that are so important that I think you should remember them, and when I do, I mark them with the Remember icon.

Whenever you may do something that could cause a major headache, I warn you with the, er, Warning icon.

Sometimes my inner geek just screams to be let out, and when it does, I have to oblige. Whenever I start veering into technical territory, I slap a big ol' Technical Stuff icon on it. If you're a geek like me (or if you're just the sort who reads every last word on every last page), I think you'll find these paragraphs interesting. If not, just move on by, confident in the knowledge that you aren't missing anything critical to the task at hand.

Where to Go from Here

If you want, you can start at the very beginning — it is, after all, a very good place to start. But you don't have to read this book from beginning to end to get what you need from it. So, make liberal use of the table of contents and the index to find exactly what you're looking for.

Want a little more guidance than that? If you're brand-new to cellphones, turn to Chapter 1. If you're interested in taking advantage of the social aspects of the phone, turn to Chapter 10. And if you're into using your phone for music and video, jump ahead to Chapter 13. If you're a hardcore gamer, advance to Chapter 16. If your boss gave you the phone and you need to get cracking, dog ear the pages starting at Chapter 20. Whatever you do, have fun with your new phone!

Part I
Getting Started

people

recent

In this part . . .

Your Windows Phone can be lots of fun and can make you very productive . . . but only if you know how to use it. Whether this is your first time using a smartphone or your first time using a touch screen, the chapters in this part give you the information you need to get started. Even veteran users of cellphones will benefit from a quick glance at the chapters in this part.

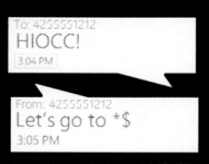

Beginning at the Beginning

Windows Phone 7 is an operating system for mobile phones. Unlike Apple's iPhone operating system, which is available only on the iPhone itself, several manufacturers will offer phones based on the Windows Phone 7 operating system, each with its own subtle variation. Microsoft has closely defined many of the key features that need to be there regardless of the manufacturer, which means that almost all the information in this book will apply to your phone, regardless of the phone manufacturer or your cellular carrier.

In this chapter, I fill you in on the basics of using your new device. You start by turning on your phone (I told you I was covering the basics!). Then I explain how cellular carriers work and tell you what to expect from your cellphone bill. I guide you through charging your phone and getting the most out of your phone's battery. I give you a basic tour of your phone's buttons and other features. And I end by telling you how to turn off your phone or put it to sleep.

 If you're not new to cellphones in general and smartphones in particular, you may want to skip this chapter. If the term *smartphone* is foreign to you, you probably haven't used one before, and reading this chapter won't hurt. A *smartphone* is a cellphone on which you can download and run applications.

First Things First: Turning On Your Phone

When you open the box with your new phone, the packaging presents you with your phone, wrapped in plastic, readily accessible. If you haven't already, take the phone out of the plastic bag and remove any protective covering material on the screen.

The On button is on the top of the phone. On the button is a symbol that looks like Figure 1-1. Press the On button for a second, and you should see the screen light up. Don't press the On button too long after the screen lights up — if you do, the phone may turn off again.

Figure 1-1: The symbol for the On button.

Your phone should arrive with enough of an electrical charge that you won't have to plug it in to an outlet right away. You can enjoy your new phone for the first day without having to charge it.

If you're used to talking on a cellphone, you may be looking for the usual wireless status bar (shown in Figure 1-2). Windows Phone 7 doesn't automatically show you the status bar. The Windows Phone 7 designers went with the philosophy that giving you visual representation only confirms what you already know by listening. Coverage for cellular networks is pretty good these days, so they made the decision to unclutter the screen and have the status bar displayed only if you want it to be. To display the status bar, tap the top of the screen with your finger. *Voilà!* The status bar appears.

The nitty-gritty of how your phone works

As soon as you turn on your phone, several things happen. As the phone is powering up, it begins transmitting information to and receiving information from nearby cellular towers. The first information exchanged includes your phone's electronic serial number. Every cellphone has its own unique serial number built in to the hardware of the phone; the serial number in current-generation cellphones can't be duplicated or used by any other phone.

The technical name of this electronic serial number depends on your cellular carrier. AT&T, T-Mobile, and U.S. Cellular call it an International Mobile Equipment Identity (IMEI) number. Verizon and Sprint refer to it as an electronic serial number (ESN).

It doesn't matter to the phone or the cellular tower if you're near your home when you turn on your phone — that's the joy of cellphones.

All the cellular networks have agreements that allow you to use cellular networks in other parts of the country and, sometimes, around the world.

That said, a call outside your cellular provider's own network may be expensive. Within the United States, many service plans allow you to pay the same rate if you use your phone anywhere in the United States to call anywhere in the United States. But if you travel outside the United States, even to Canada, you may end up paying through the nose. **Remember:** Before you leave on a trip, check with your cellular carrier about your rates. Even if you travel internationally only a few times every year, a different service plan may work better for you. Your cellular carrier can fill you in on your options. For more on billing, check out the section "You and Your Shadow: Understanding How Your Cellular Carrier Bills You" in this chapter.

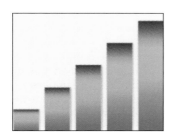

Figure 1-2: How many bars do you have?

You and Your Shadow: Understanding How Your Cellular Carrier Bills You

In the United States, most cellular companies sell phones at a significant discount when you sign up for a service agreement. And most cellular companies offer discounts on phones when you want to upgrade to something newer (as long as you also sign up for another couple years of service). So, it's not surprising that most people buy their phones directly from cellular companies.

If your new Windows Phone 7 device is an upgrade from an older phone, you may have a service plan that was suitable with your last phone but isn't so great anymore. If this is your first cellphone (ever, or with this particular carrier), you may have started on an entry-level plan, thinking you wouldn't need that many minutes, only to find that you and your phone are inseparable and you need a better plan. The good news is that most cellular carriers allow you to change your service plan.

Most cellular service plans have three components:

 ✔ Voice usage
 ✔ Text usage
 ✔ Data usage

I walk you through each of these components — and how Windows Phone 7 affects them — in the following sections.

Voice usage

Voice usage is the most costly and the most complex element of most service plans. Cellular providers typically offer plans with a certain number of anytime minutes and a certain number of night/weekend minutes. Some providers offer plans with reduced rates (or even free calls) to frequently called numbers, to other cellphones with the same cellular provider, or to other cellphones in general. If you talk a lot, you may be able to opt for an unlimited voice plan (for domestic calls only).

At its core, a Windows Phone 7 device is, obviously, a phone. In the early days of smartphones, manufacturers were stung by the criticism that smartphones weren't as easy to use as traditional cellphones. Indeed, you do have to bring up the Phone screen to make a call (more on making and receiving calls in Chapter 2). To avoid this criticism, Microsoft has made sure that the screen used to make calls is only two clicks away from the *Start screen* (what you see after the phone is ready for you to start using it).

One way that Windows Phone 7 devices differ from other smartphones is that you can set up a page for some of your favorite people to keep track of their e-mails, texts, and entries on their social networking sites (see Part IV). When you read a message or an interesting entry, you may be more inclined to call that person — which may be a good thing or a bad thing, depending on how many minutes you have on your calling plan.

Text usage

Some service plans include unlimited texting; others offer a certain number of text messages for a flat rate. A texting bundle is an add-on to your voice plan. For example, you may pay an additional $5 per month to get 200 free text messages; that means you can send and receive a total of 200 messages per month. If you go over that limit, you pay a certain amount per message (usually more for text messages you send than those you receive).

As with voice, the Windows Phone 7 operating system makes it convenient to text, but it doesn't obligate you to buy a text plan. You can make phone calls regardless of whether you have a text plan.

At the same time, texting is so darn convenient when you just want to get or send a little bit of information. Plus, it's being built in to many of the communications tools that will be part of your phone. Although your Windows Phone manages the technical interfaces, you may end up sending and receiving more texts than you expect.

My advice is to get at least some texting, and be ready to decide whether you want to pay for more or stay with a minimal plan and budget your texts.

Data usage

Access to the Internet is essential to get the full experience of Windows Phone 7. The Internet is where you access all the capabilities that make the Windows Phone 7 so special.

Paying for the Internet on your Windows Phone is similar to paying your Internet service provider for Internet access for your PC at home. Although you can use Wi-Fi to supplement the coverage you get from your cellular carrier, you need to have a data plan from your cellular carrier as well. There's no getting around it with your Windows Phone.

Most cellular companies price Internet access with one flat rate. So, when you get a Window Phone 7 device, you'll pay a certain amount per month for data usage (access to the Internet), and it doesn't matter how much you use (or don't use) the Internet on your phone — you still pay that same flat rate.

What if I didn't get my phone from a cellular company?

With a few exceptions (such as an unlocked GSM phone), each phone is associated with a particular cellular company. Maybe you bought a secondhand phone on eBay or you got a phone from a friend who didn't want his anymore. If you didn't get your phone directly from a cellular provider, you need to figure out which provider the phone is associated with and get a service plan from that company. Usually, you'll see the company's logo on the phone somewhere. If you don't know what carrier the phone was associated with and no logo is on the phone, you need to find out which carrier the phone is set to work with. The quickest way is to take the phone to any cellular store — they know how to figure it out.

If you want to narrow down the possibilities on your own, you need to do some investigation. The easiest way is to take off the back of the phone to find the plate with the model and serial number for the phone. If you see IMEI on the plate, the phone is based on a technology called Global System for Mobile (GSM); it'll work with either AT&T or T-Mobile (or both). If you see ESN on the plate, the phone will work with either Verizon or Sprint (but not both).

This is good news: As you customize your phone to keep up with your friends and access your favorite sites, the cost of access won't increase. (Of course, the downside is that, if you use the Internet on your phone only a tiny bit, you can't get a cheaper data plan. But then you probably wouldn't be buying a Windows Phone 7 device in that case. Even still, many new smartphone users face sticker shock with their new data plan. Be ready and recognize that it will be worth it!)

More good news is that your cellular carrier has good data coverage. It isn't perfect, but it's much better than if you were to try to rely on free Wi-Fi hotspots.

Of course, some Web-based services may charge subscription fees. For example, WeatherBug (www.weatherbug.com) tells you weather conditions for free, but it also offers WeatherBug Professional, which provides more information for a monthly fee. If you want WeatherBug Professional on your phone, you have to pay the piper. The good news is that some of these services can be billed through your cellular carrier if you want. Check with your carrier.

Charging Your Phone and Managing Battery Life

Windows Phones use lithium-ion batteries. Although you probably don't have to plug it in to an outlet right away, the first time you do plug it in, you should allow it to charge overnight.

You'll hear all kinds of "battery lore" out there that's left over from earlier battery technologies. For example, lithium-ion batteries don't have a "memory" like NiCad batteries did. So, you don't have to be careful to allow the battery to fully discharge before recharging it.

Your phone comes with at least one battery charger. When it comes to charging, Windows Phone 7 devices can be very different from one manufacturer and cellular carrier to the next. In addition to the battery charger that comes in the box with the phone, you may have several other charging options:

- ✐ **Wall charger:** A wall charger plugs in to the power port on your phone and allows you to charge the phone from a standard electrical outlet.

    Unplug the battery charger when you aren't charging your phone. If you leave the charger plugged in, there will be a small but continuous draw of power.

- ✐ **Travel charger:** What distinguishes a travel charger from a regular wall charger is that the prongs fold in to the *wall bug* (the plug that you stick into the outlet). Some manufacturers ship a travel charger with the phone; others don't.

- ✐ **Car charger:** A car charger lets you charge your phone from an outlet in your car (sometimes from your cigarette lighter).

- ✐ **Fuel cell or photocell charger:** Several companies make products that can charge your phone if you don't have access to a wall outlet or a car outlet.

Only buy a charger that is designed to work with your Windows Phone and that comes from a reputable manufacturer. A cheaper alternative to what you can buy at the cellular store is not necessarily a bargain. Cheap chargers may physically fit in the charging port on your phone and may charge the phone, but lithium-ion batteries are sensitive to voltage, and your off-brand charger may hurt the performance of your battery.

High heat shortens the life of your battery. Be careful not to leave your phone on your car's dashboard. In general, if you keep your phone with you — except when you sit in a sauna or sweat lodge — you'll be safe.

If you take good care of it, your battery should last about two years with a drop in performance of about 25 percent from the condition it was in when you took it out of the box. At that point, you can replace the battery or upgrade to the newest Windows Phone.

Navigating around the Phone

Windows Phone 7 devices differ from other smartphones in that Windows Phones have significantly fewer hardware buttons. In their place is a much heavier reliance on buttons on the screen.

In this section, I guide you through your phone's buttons, touch screen, and keyboard.

The phone's buttons

Microsoft has reduced the number of hardware buttons on the Windows Phone 7 device to six, unless the phone has a keyboard. I cover them all in the following sections.

Buttons on the front

Beneath the Start screen are three buttons that you use to control what appears on the screen. From left to right, they are the Back button, the Start button, and the Search button (see Figure 1-3).

The Back button

The Back button on your phone is similar to the Back button in your Web browser on your computer. As you start navigating through the screens on your phone, pressing the Back button takes you back to the previous screen. If you keep pressing the Back button, eventually you'll get to the Start screen. Figure 1-4 shows a couple of the options for what the Back button may look like on your phone.

The Start button

Pressing the Start button takes you directly to the Start screen. The icon, shown in Figure 1-5, is a silhouette of the familiar Windows icon.

The Start button comes in handy when you want to change what you're doing with the phone, such as going from browsing the Web to making a phone call.

The Search button

Use the Search button to find information on your device. The icon is shown in Figure 1-6.

Courtesy of Microsoft Corporation
Figure 1-3: The Windows Phone 7 Start screen.

Figure 1-4: The Back button looks something like this.

Figure 1-5: The Start button takes you to the Start screen.

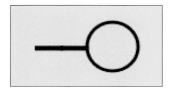

Figure 1-6: The Search button looks like this.

When you press the Search button, a Search screen pops up along with a small software keyboard (see Figure 1-7) so that you can enter the text to describe what you want to search for.

The search is based on the application you're using at the moment. If you're in the phone application, the Search button searches your telephone book for a contact based on the text you enter. If you're on the Internet, it searches the Web. If you're on the Start screen, it searches the whole phone.

Turn to the section "The keyboard," later in this chapter, for more on the ways you can enter your search terms.

Side buttons

In addition to the three buttons on the front, there are three buttons on the side of the phone: the Power button, the Camera button, and the Volume button.

Courtesy of Microsoft Corporation

Figure 1-7: Use the software keyboard to search for the information you need.

The Power button

The Power button is on top of the phone. In addition to powering up the phone, it puts the device into sleep mode if you press it for a moment while the phone is on.

Sleep mode shuts off the screen, suspends any running applications, and turns off the radios in the phone. The advantage of Sleep mode (over completely turning off the phone) is that hitting any of the hardware buttons wakes up the phone — it's ready to operate in just a few seconds. If you turn off the phone, it takes longer to start back up.

You can't receive any calls while your phone is in sleep mode.

Sleep mode is different from what happens when you haven't used the phone in a little while. After 15 or 20 seconds, the screen turns off. The screen is the biggest user of power on the device. Having it go dark saves a large amount of battery life. However, the phone is still alert to any incoming calls — if someone calls you, the screen automatically lights up.

Sleep mode barely uses any power, so it will not affect your battery life. Only use sleep mode if you don't want to be disturbed by calls. Otherwise, just leave your phone alone and it will simply shut off the screen to preserve battery life.

The Camera button

The digital camera is among the most popular features on cellular phones. The camera may vary from one manufacturer and cellular carrier to the next, but Microsoft has set a minimum standard of 5 megapixels and a flash; your phone may have higher resolution.

What does *not* vary is that pressing the Camera button launches the Camera application. Also, after the Camera application is up, you press the Camera button to take a picture.

The Volume button

Technically, there are two Volume buttons — one to increase the volume and the other to lower it. The Volume buttons control the volume of all the audio sources on the phone, including the following:

- The phone ringer for when a call comes in
- The phone headset when you're talking on the phone
- The volume from the digital music and video player

The Volume buttons are "aware" of the context of what volume you're changing. If you're listening to music, they raise or lower the music volume but leave the ringer and phone earpiece volumes unchanged.

The Volume buttons complement software settings you can make within the applications. For example, you can open the music player software and increase the volume on the appropriate screen. Then you can use the hardware buttons to decrease the volume and you'll see the volume setting on the screen go down.

The touch screen

To cram the information that you need onto one screen, Microsoft takes a radical approach to screen layout. To make this new approach work, there are several finger motions that you'll want to become familiar with to work with your screen. I cover these motions in the following sections.

Tapping to select or launch from the screen

A *tap* is simply a touch of the screen. Tapping is much like using a touch screen at a retail kiosk. Figure 1-8 shows what the motion should look like.

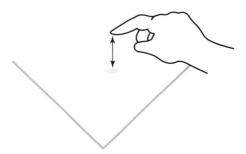

Single touch of the screen.
Finger down on a single point within a bounded area and back up within a short period of time.

Figure 1-8: The tap motion.

In some ways, the tap is like a single click of a mouse on a computer screen. It allows you to select options on a screen.

One difference between a mouse on a computer and a tap on a Windows Phone is that it takes a double-click to open an application on your computer, but only a single tap to open an application on your Windows Phone.

Don't press and hold. If you leave your finger on the screen for more than an instant, the phone gets confused and thinks that you want to do something more.

Moving around the screen "behind" the screen

The other finger actions help you move around the screen to get to the information you need at the screen resolution that you want.

You can set your computer to whatever screen resolution you like. And you may have noticed, if you used a friend's computer with a different screen resolution, that the layout of the buttons is a little different. What's happening is that the software is sized to on the resolution of your screen. To access what is not immediately visible on your screen, you've probably worked with a scroll bar, like the horizontal scroll bar shown in Figure 1-9.

Figure 1-9: A horizontal scroll bar on a computer.

To overcome the practical realities of screen size on a phone that will fit into your pocket, the Windows Phone embraces a panorama screen layout. Figure 1-10 represents a panorama screen layout. The full width of the screen is accessible, but only the part bounded by the screen of the Windows Phone is visible on the display.

Courtesy of Microsoft Corporation

Figure 1-10: The Windows Phone 7 panorama display.

To see more of the screen, you have several choices: pan, flicks, pinch and stretch, and double taps. I cover all these in the following sections.

Pan

The simplest finger motion on the phone is the *pan*. You place your finger on a point on the screen and your finger drags the image on the screen until you lift your finger. Figure 1-11 shows what the motion looks like.

The pan motion allows you to move slowly around the panorama. This motion is like clicking on the scroll bar and moving it slowly.

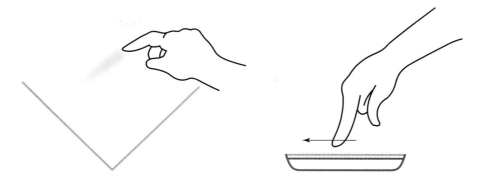

Finger down followed by finger move in a single or multiple
directions. Pan ends on finger up (or when another gesture starts).

Figure 1-11: The pan motion for controlled movement.

Flicks

To move quickly around the panorama, you can flick (see Figure 1-12).

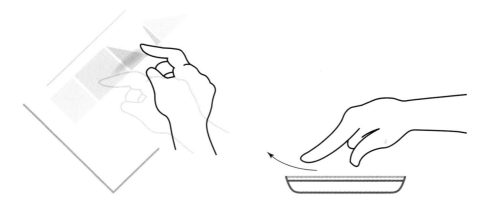

Finger down followed by a quick finger move in a single
direction and finger up. Flick can also follow a pan gesture.

Figure 1-12: The flick motion for faster movement.

Better control of this motion will come with practice. The stronger the flick,
the more the panorama will move.

Pinch and stretch

Zoom options change the magnification of the area on the screen. You can zoom out to see more features at a smaller size, or zoom in to see more detail at a larger size.

To zoom out, you put two fingers on the screen and pinch the image. The pinch motion is shows in Figure 1-13.

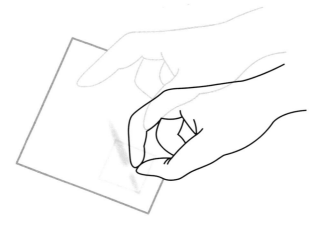

Figure 1-13: Use the pinch motion to zoom out.

The opposite motion is to zoom in. This involves the stretch motion, as shown in Figure 1-14.

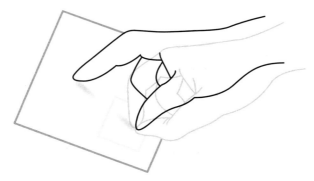

Figure 1-14: Use the stretch motion to zoom in.

Although pinch and stretch work with panoramas, these motions are most useful when you're in applications that aren't sized for your screen, such as Web pages. However, you can use them wherever you like.

Double tap

The double tap (shown in Figure 1-15) is where you touch the same button on the screen twice in rapid succession. You use the double tap to jump between a zoomed-in and a zoomed-out image to get you back to the previous resolution. This option saves you from any frustration in getting back to a familiar perspective.

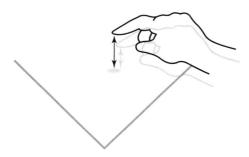

Two quick taps within a bounded area.

Figure 1-15: The double-tap motion.

It's important to time the taps so that the phone doesn't interpret them as two separate taps. With a little practice, you'll get the timing of the second tap down.

The keyboard

The screen of the Windows Phone is important, but you'll still probably spend more time on the keyboard entering data on a small QWERTY keyboard. All Windows Phones come with a software keyboard; some come with a software keyboard *and* a hardware keyboard.

Tapping on the software keyboard

The software keyboard automatically pops up when the application detects that there is a need for user text input. The keyboard in Figure 1-16 appears at the bottom of the screen.

Figure 1-16: The software keyboard.

For example, if you're searching for the Seattle Art Museum within Seattle on Bing Maps, you tap the Search button, and the keyboard in Figure 1-16 will pop up on the screen, as shown in Figure 1-17.

In this case, a text box pops up in addition to the keyboard. As you tap out "Seattle Art Museum," the text appears in the box on the screen as if you had typed it on a hardware keyboard. When you tap the Search button, the keyboard disappears and the location of the Seattle Art Museum is highlighted on your phone. The phone is smart enough to know when the keyboard should appear and disappear.

If you find that your software-only keyboard is frustrating, many cellular carriers offer a trade-in program. If you return your phone to the store within a limited time, such as 30 days, they'll exchange it for a model with a built-in hardware keyboard.

If your phone has a hardware keyboard, the software keyboard doesn't pop up automatically.

Thumbing on your hardware keyboard

Some Windows Phone models have a slide-out keyboard. The advantage of a hardware keyboard is that it offers more tactile feedback than a touch screen. You may prefer this as an alternative to only having the software keyboard.

If you have a hardware keyboard but find that you are happiest using the software keyboard, you may be able to take advantage of a trade-in program and get a Windows Phone without a hardware keyboard.

Figure 1-17: The software keyboard on the screen of a map.

Turning Off the Phone

You can leave your phone on every minute until you're ready to upgrade to the newest Windows Phone in a few years. You can also put it to sleep overnight, several days, or even longer (see "The Power button," earlier in this chapter, for more on sleep mode).

But sometimes it's best to simply shut down the phone if you aren't going to use it for several days or more. To shut down the phone completely, simply press and hold the power button for 5 seconds.

2

Making Your First Call

In This Chapter

▶ Dialing and answering phone calls

▶ Using your call list

▶ Making emergency calls

▶ Connecting to a Bluetooth headset

*A*t its essence, any cellphone — no matter how fancy or smart — exists to make phone calls. The good news is that making and receiving phone calls on the Windows Phone is very easy. This chapter describes the process.

In this chapter, I also show you how you can use your call list to keep track of your calls. Many people have cellphones at least in part for emergencies, so you'll be glad to know that, in this chapter, I tell you how to call for help when you need it.

Finally, if you're like many people, you're never doing just one thing at a time, and a Bluetooth headset can make it easier for you to talk on the phone while driving, wrangling kids and dogs, or just plain living life. In this chapter, I show you how to hook up your phone to a Bluetooth headset so you can make and receive phone calls hands-free.

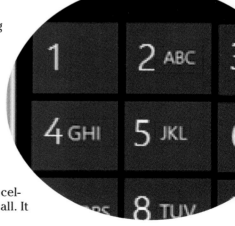

Making Your First Call

After your phone is on and you're connected to your cellular carrier (see Chapter 1), you can make a phone call. It all starts from the Start screen (shown in Figure 2-1).

Courtesy of Microsoft Corporation

Figure 2-1: The Start screen on a Windows Phone is where you begin making a call.

In Windows Phone 7, the Start screen is set up a little differently from most of the other screens. Its panorama is vertical, rather than horizontal. (Refer to Chapter 1 for more on this panorama effect.)

In Figure 2-1, you see four blue squares that have icons on them. In the Windows Phone 7 lexicon, these squares are called *tiles*. Tiles are an important feature of the Start screen. They allow you access many of the features of the phone, and you can set them up so that navigating to your favorite phone services is easy. (For more on customizing your tiles, turn to Chapter 22.)

To make a call, you start by tapping the Phone tile (see Figure 2-2). Tapping the Phone tile takes you to the Call History Phone screen (shown in Figure 2-3). From this screen, you tap on the phone icon to get to the Dialer screen (shown in Figure 2-4).

Courtesy of Microsoft Corporation

Figure 2-2: Tap the Phone tile on the Start screen to get to the Call History screen.

You dial the phone by tapping the telephone number you want to reach. (You don't need to dial 1 before the area code — just dial the area code and the seven-digit number.) Then tap the Call button at the bottom of the screen to place the call. Within a few seconds, you should hear the phone ringing at the other end.

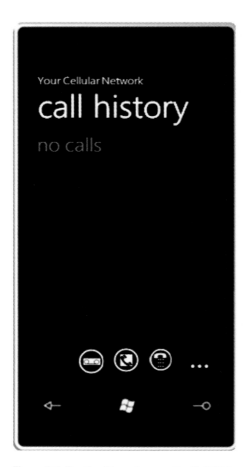

Figure 2-3: Tap the Phone icon on the Call History
screen to make a call.

When you're done with your call, tap the End button at the bottom of the
screen, and the call will be disconnected.

Figure 2-4: The Dialer screen is where you dial the number you want to call.

Receiving Your First Call

Receiving a call is even easier than making a call. When someone calls your cellular number for the first time, his caller ID information will appear along with two buttons: Answer and Ignore.

This is what happens when your phone is new. In Part IV, I fill you in on some exciting options that you can enable (or not) when you get a call. For example, you can specify a unique ringtone for a particular number or have an image of the caller pop up on the screen.

If you tap the Answer button, whatever you were doing on the phone — such as listening to music or playing a game — will be suspended until the call is over. You end the call by tapping the End button, and the game or application you were using will pick up where you left off.

If you tap the Ignore button, the caller is sent to your voicemail, where he can leave a message or just hang up.

In order for callers to be able to leave you voicemail messages, you must set up your voicemail. If you haven't yet set up your voicemail, the caller will hear a recorded message saying that your voicemail account is not yet set up. Some cellular carriers can set up voicemail for you when you activate the account and get the phone; others require you to set up voicemail on your own. You can ask about this when you get your phone. Otherwise, information that explains how to set up voicemail should be included with the phone.

The Call History: Keeping Track of Your Calls

One of the nice features of cellular phones is that the phone keeps a record of the calls that you've made and received. Sure, you may have caller ID on your land line at home or work, but land-line phones don't keep track of who you've called. Cellphones, on the other hand, keep track of all the numbers you've called. This information can be very convenient — for example, if you want to call someone you just called and you don't have her number handy.

The call list is categorized as follows:

- ✒ Incoming calls
- ✒ Outgoing calls
- ✒ All calls (incoming and outgoing)

You can access these lists by tapping the ellipsis (. . .) on the bottom-right corner of the screen. Tapping the ellipsis brings up the call history (shown in Figure 2-5).

Windows Phone 7 frequently uses the ellipsis as a symbol to mean, "Tap here to bring up more options."

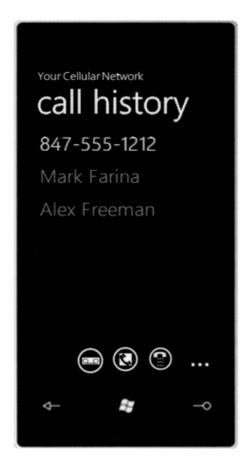

Figure 2-5: Call lists keep track of all your incoming and outgoing calls.

You can tap any number on the call list, and it appears on the Phone screen. If you want to call that number, tap Call.

Emergency Calls: The 411 on 911

Cellphones are wonderful tools for calling for help in an emergency. Windows Phones, like all cellphones in the United States, can make emergency calls to 911 even if the phone isn't registered with a cellular carrier.

When you accidentally dial 911

If you accidentally dial 911 from your Windows Phone, don't hang up. Just tell the operator that it was an accidental call. She may ask some questions to verify that you are, indeed, safe and not being forced to say that your call was an accident.

If you panic and hang up after accidentally dialing 911, you'll get a call from the nearest 911 call center. Answer the call, even if you feel foolish. If you don't answer the call, the 911 call center will assume you're in trouble and can't respond. They'll track you down from the GPS in your phone to verify that you're safe. If you thought you'd feel foolish explaining your mistake to a 911 operator, imagine how foolish you'd feel explaining it to the police officer who tracks you down.

If you need to dial 911, tap the Phone tile on the Start screen. Then tap the numbers 911, and hit Call. You'll be routed to the 911 call center nearest to your location. This works even if you're traveling. So, if you live in Chicago, and you get in a car accident in Charlotte, when you dial 911, you're connected to the 911 call center in Charlotte.

There is an Emergency Number button on the dial pad. You can tap that and be connected to the local 911 call center.

When you call 911 from a land line, the address you're calling from is usually displayed for the operator, but when you're calling from a cellphone, the operator doesn't have that specific information. So, when you call 911, the operator may say, "911. *Where* is your emergency?" This question may throw you, because you're probably focused on *what* is happening and not on *where*. Take a moment and come up with a good description of where you are — the street you're on, the nearest cross street (if you know it), any businesses or other landmarks nearby. When the operator knows where you are, she's in a better position to help you with the problem.

Synching a Bluetooth Headset

A Bluetooth headset is a device that allows you to talk on your phone without holding the phone up to your head and without any cords running from the phone to your earpiece. You've probably come across plenty of people talking on Bluetooth headsets. You may even have wondered if they were a little crazy, talking to themselves. Well, call yourself crazy now, because when you start using a Bluetooth headset, you may never want to go back.

Not surprisingly, Windows Phones can connect to Bluetooth headsets. The first step to using a Bluetooth headset with your phone is to synch the two devices. Here's how:

1. **From the Start screen on your phone, pan one screen to the right by sliding your finger across the screen.**

   This gets you to the Bluetooth icon.

2. **Tap the Bluetooth icon.**

   Here you can make changes to the Bluetooth settings on your device.

3. **Tap the Add New Device icon.**

   You will see an indicator that your phone is looking for another device.

4. **Put your headset into synching mode.**

   Follow the instructions that came with your headset.

5. **Tap the Synch icon.**

   After a moment, the phone will "see" the headset. When it does, it asks you to enter the security code and the software keyboard will pop up. Enter the security code for your headset, and tap the Enter button.

   The security code on most headsets is 0000, but check the instructions that came with your headset if that doesn't work.

Your headset is now synched to your phone.

3

The Joy of Text

In This Chapter

▶ Sending a text message

▶ Sending a text message with an attachment

▶ Receiving a text message

▶ Reviewing your old text messages

Sure, cellphones were made for talking. But these days, many people use their cellphones even more for texting. *Text messages* (short messages, usually 160 characters or less, sent by cellphone) are particularly convenient when you can't talk at the moment (maybe you're in a meeting or class) or when you just have a small bit of information to share (for example, "Running late — see you soon!").

Many cellphone users — particularly younger ones — prefer sending texts to making a phone call. They find texting a faster and more convenient way to communicate, and they often use a texting shorthand to fit more "content" in that character limit.

Windows Phone 7 makes sending and receiving text messages convenient — whether you're an occasional or pathological texter. In this chapter, I fill you in on how to send a text message (with or without an attachment), how to receive a text message, and how to read your old text messages.

Sending Your First Text

When you're ready to brag about your new Windows Phone, send a text:

1. On the Start screen, tap the Text tile (shown in Figure 3-1).

The number on this tile tells you how many new texts you've stored on the phone.

The first screen is Messaging Conversations (see Figure 3-2).

At the bottom of the Messaging Conversations screen is an icon of a plus sign in a circle (see Figure 3-3).

2. Tap the plus sign.

The Text screen (shown in Figure 3-4) appears. You see a text box at the top, and a keyboard at the bottom.

Courtesy of Microsoft Corporation

Figure 3-1: The Text tile on the Start screen tells you how many new texts you have.

Figure 3-2: The Messaging Conversations screen.

Figure 3-3: Tapping the plus
sign starts a new text.

Figure 3-4: The Text screen.

3. **Tap in the ten-digit mobile telephone number of the recipient.**

   A text box in the shape of a text balloon in a cartoon pops up on the screen. The keyboard remains on the bottom of the screen.

4. **Start tapping the message you want to send, and it appears in the text balloon.**

   Your text message can be up to 160 characters, including spaces and punctuation. To assist you in making things go faster, your Windows Phone automatically suggests completed words based on what you've already typed in. For example, in Figure 3-5, the phone is guessing that you may have wanted to type "Rust," "Ghat," "That's" or "That'll."

The phone takes it from here. Within a few seconds, the message is sent to your friend's cellphone.

Figure 3-5: The Text screen with word completion.

You can select one of the guesses by tapping on that word, or you can ignore it and continue tapping in the word you want yourself.

5. **After you've finished your message, send the text by tapping the button that looks like Figure 3-6.**

Figure 3-6: Press this button to send your text.

Sending an Attachment with a Text

What if you want to send something in addition to or instead of text? What if, say, you want to send a picture, some music, or a Word document along with your text? Easy . . . as long as the phone on the receiving end can recognize the attachment!

Before you send your text, tap the Attach button (see Figure 3-7). You'll be asked what file you want to attach, and you'll be able to search for the file. After you've selected the file, tap Done, and the attachment becomes a part of your text message. If you need to continue typing your text message, you can. When you're done with the text portion of the message, tap the Send Text button, and off it goes.

Figure 3-7: Press this button to attach something to your text.

A simple text message is an SMS message. *SMS* stands for "short message service." When you add an attachment, you're sending an *MMS* message; MMS stands for "multimedia messaging service." Back in the day, MMS messages cost more to send and receive than SMS messages did. These days, that isn't the case in the United States.

Receiving Your First Text

Receiving a text is even easier than sending one.

When you're having a text conversation and you receive a new text from the person you're texting with, your phone displays it in its own text bubble. In Figure 3-8, your original message is at the top, and the message you've just received is on the bottom, so you can see the conversation you're having.

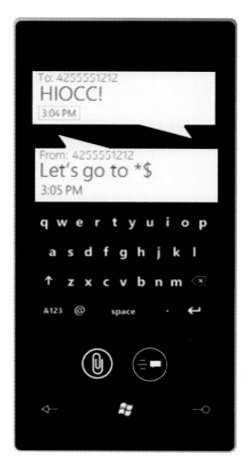

Figure 3-8: A text conversation.

Each message is time-stamped and kept in order. Conversations aren't always text and response — people sometimes send several texts before the other party replies. The orientation of the bubbles is a visual clue to keep straight which message is from who — the ones you've sent have the bubble going up (like a cartoon bubble would be when positioned over the person's head), and the ones you've received have the bubble going down (like a cartoon bubble positioned below a person's head).

If you aren't an experienced texter, here's a clue to what the messages in Figure 3-8 are saying: HIOOC is an acronym that stands for, "Help! I'm out of coffee!" The reply is "Let's go to *$" (* = Star and $ = bucks). Of course, you don't have to talk in acronyms to send texts.

The previous example assumes that you're ready to have a text conversation. That isn't always the case, though. Sometimes, the text arrives in your inbox. To access the text, press the Windows button on your phone to get to the Start screen (refer to Figure 3-1), where you see a number on the Text tile. This tells you the number of unread texts you have. In the case of your first text, the number on the tile would switch from 0 to 1. To view the text, tap the Text tile. This takes you to the Messaging Conversations screen (refer to Figure 3-2). The first several characters of the received text are displayed on the screen. To read all the text, tap on that message.

Managing Your Text History

The Messaging Conversations screen stores and organizes all your texts until you delete them. You'll want to clean up this screen every now and then.

The simplest option for managing your messages is to tap the ellipsis (. . .) on the lower-right corner of the screen. Here you're given options for managing your texts.

You can delete the older texts and conversations. You can also delete all messages. Trust me, deleting all your message can be cathartic!

Part II
Moving Beyond the Basics

The 5th Wave

By Rich Tennant

PCS PHONES

"So, what kind of roaming capabilities does this thing have?"

In this part . . .

You can use your Windows Phone to do all kinds of things, from the obvious (like making calls and texting) to the super-cool (like playing HD radio, playing games on Xbox LIVE, and accessing all your digital calendars on one screen). This part fills you in on your options so you can prioritize what you want to do. When you're learning about your phone, the goal is to avoid information overload and focus first on the things you're most excited about.

I don't just cover the fancy stuff, though. In this part, I also introduce you to some of the features that come standard with your phone. Sure, there are dozens of capabilities you can add to your phone, but before you get into those, it helps to know what you already have.

4

What You Can Do with Your Phone

In This Chapter

▶ Reviewing the basic capabilities of just about any cellphone

▶ Understanding what sets smartphones apart

▶ Mapping out what makes Windows Phone 7 so cool

*W*hether you want just the basics out of your phone — the ability to make and take phone calls, customize your ringtone, take some pictures, maybe use a Bluetooth headset — or you want your phone to be always by your side, a tool for multiple uses all throughout your day, you can make that happen. In this chapter, I outline all the things your phone can do — from the basics, to what makes Windows Phones different from the rest. Throughout the remainder of the book, I walk you through the steps you need to take to get your phone doing what makes you the happiest.

The Basics: What Any Cellphone Can Do (And How the Windows Phone Does It)

Most entry-level cellphones on the market today include some basic functionalities, and it probably comes as no surprise to you that Microsoft has included all these basic capabilities in your Windows Phone. In addition to making and taking calls (see Chapter 2) and sending and receiving texts (see Chapter 3), your phone has the following basic features:

✔ **Digital camera:** The lowest-resolution Windows Phone is 5 megapixels. Your phone may have more, but 5 megapixels is more than enough for posting good-quality images on the Internet.

> ✔ **Photos:** The Windows Phone allows you to manage your photos, including which one you use as a background image on your Start screen.
>
> ✔ **Ringtones:** You can replace the standard ringtone with custom ringtones that you download to your phone. You also can specify different rings for different numbers.
>
> ✔ **Bluetooth:** The Windows Phone specifications set by Microsoft ensure that your phone supports stereo and standard Bluetooth devices. (See Chapter 2 for more on Bluetooth.)
>
> ✔ **High-resolution touch screen:** The Windows Phone offers one of the highest-resolution touch screens on the market (480 x 800 pixels versus 320 x 480 for iPhone 3Gs).

What Makes a Smartphone Smart

In addition to the basic capabilities of any entry-level cellphone, the Windows Phone has capabilities associated with many popular smartphones, such as Apple's iPhone and the phones based on Google's Android operating system. These include the following:

> ✔ **Internet access:** The ability to access Web sites through a Web browser on your phone
>
> ✔ **Wireless e-mail:** The ability to send and receive e-mail from your phone
>
> ✔ **Multimedia:** The ability to play music and videos on your phone
>
> ✔ **Downloaded games and applications:** The ability to run games and applications you buy from an online software marketplace

I discuss these four capabilities in greater detail in the following sections.

Internet access

Until a few years ago, the only way to access the Internet when you were away from a desk was with a laptop. Laptops are great, but they weigh at least a few pounds and need time to boot up. Plus, lugging a laptop around with you everywhere you go just isn't very practical — and it's not like the whole world is one big Wi-Fi hotspot.

Smartphones are a great alternative to laptops because they're small, convenient, and ready to launch their Web browsers right away. Even more important, when you have a smartphone, you can access the Internet wherever you are — regardless of whether Wi-Fi is available. The drawback to smartphones is that their screen resolution is less than even the most basic laptop screen. Plus, image-heavy Web sites can take a long time to load.

To accommodate this problem, more Web sites are adding mobile versions. These sites are slimmed-down versions of their main site — they have fewer images, but offer similar access to the information on the site.

Figure 4-1 shows the regular Web site for refdesk.com. Figure 4-2 shows its mobilized version. The mobilized version has fewer pictures and is more vertically oriented.

Figure 4-1: The main Web site is wider and has more images.

Fact Checker for the Internet

MOBILE REFDESK

Thursday, April 29, 2010

- Fact of the Day
- Site of the Day
- Thought of the Day

- DOW | Crude | Gas | Money
- Google Calendar

INTERNET SEARCH:
- Google Search
- MSN Live Search
- Yahoo Search

TOP HEADLINES:
- AP | Reuters
- ABC | CBS | CNN
- FOX | MSNBC | NPR
- NYT | USA Today | Wash. Post

MORE NEWS:
- Google News Headlines
- Yahoo News Headlines
- Business Headlines
- Entertainment Headlines
- Sci/Tech Headlines
- ESPN Sports
- Latest Weather

FEATURES:
- Essential Mobile Web Sites
- Reference Resources
- Today's Pictures
- Daily Diversions
- Just For Fun
- Newspaper and Media News Sites

© Refdesk.com™ 2009

157,417

Figure 4-2: A mobile Web site is a slimmed-down version of the main site.

The Apple iPhone was the first smartphone to offer multi-touch capability, which allows you to zoom in and out by pinching or stretching (see Chapter 1). Today, the Windows Phone offers the same capability. On the Windows Phone, you can use the mobile version of a Web site if you want, but if you prefer to use the standard Web site, you can pinch and stretch your way to get the information you want.

For more information on accessing the Internet from your Windows Phone, turn to Chapter 6.

Wireless e-mail

The Blackberry from Research In Motion hit the cellular phone market in 2001, and wireless e-mail has been growing by double and triple digits ever since. On your smartphone, you can access your business and personal e-mail accounts, reading and sending e-mail messages on the go. Depending on your e-mail system, you may be able to set it up so that, when you delete an e-mail on your phone, the e-mail is deleted on your computer at the same time, so you don't have to read the same messages on your phone and your computer.

Chapter 11 covers setting up your business and personal e-mail accounts.

Multimedia

Some smartphones allow you to play music and videos on your phone in place of a dedicated MP3 or video player. Your Windows Phone is no exception. On the Windows Phone, you use Microsoft's Zune services to access music and videos. (For more on Zune, check out the nearby sidebar, "The history of Zune.")

Part V covers how to use the Zune services with your Windows Phone.

Downloaded games and applications

Most smartphones can run games and applications that you can buy from an online software marketplace. Microsoft is working with application developers —large and small — to offer a variety of applications and games for the Windows Phone available exclusively on the Windows Phone Marketplace (`http://marketplace.windowsphone.com`). New applications are constantly being developed, so check back regularly.

For more information on downloading games and applications, turn to Chapters 8 and 9.

The history of Zune

The first digital music player, generically called an MP3 player, was launched in 2001. Over the next several years, Apple's iPod was the market leader because it had an easy user interface and a convenient store, iTunes, where people could acquire their music.

Microsoft launched its MP3 player, the Zune, along with the Zune music store, in November 2006. The Zune was different from the iPod in that it also incorporated an FM radio and could accept software upgrades that would offer different, and presumably better, screens. What also distinguished the Zune from other MP3 players, like the iPod, is what Microsoft called the "social" aspects of music. There were chat groups on the Zune Web site for fans of a particular genre of music. In addition, you could share tracks with a limited number of friends for a specified number of plays or a few days.

Later, the Zune Web site (www.zune.net), the only source of music for Zune players, offered lower-cost pricing options than were available on the much larger iTunes site. Rather than a standard 99¢ per track, you could access the entire library of songs for a flat rate of $15 per month, plus you could keep up to ten tracks indefinitely if you let your subscription lapse.

In addition to this nice licensing program, Microsoft launched the Zune HD, a device that had the technical ability (with the right connectors) to store and play a full-length movie in HD format. Zune HD was much more powerful and appealing than other MP3 players because of its super-slick user interface. Haven't seen a Zune HD? Don't worry — it's virtually identical to what's on your Windows Phone. In a way, the Windows Phone 7 is a Zune HD cellphone.

What Your Windows Phone 7 Can Do

Your Windows Phone is a smartphone (as described in the preceding section), but it's more than your average smartphone. It has unique capabilities and features that put it in a category all its own. In this section, I fill you in on the details.

People and social networks

One way that Windows Phone 7 is different from other smartphones is the way it allows you to put all the information on your contacts in one spot. Your Windows Phone ties together all the methods you use to communicate with the important people in your life into a single access point.

There are two ways the Windows Phone allows you to keep in touch with the people who are important to you:

✔ **You can set up a tile on your Start screen for each of the most important people in your life.** You can even set it up so that each person's image is on his unique tile. Then, when you tap on a person's tile, you see all the current messages from and to that person (whether those are e-mails, texts, voicemails, or Facebook updates, and so on). You also see all the ways that you can communicate with that person. (See Chapter 10 for more information.)

✔ **You can use the People hub.** One way to look at the People hub is like a contact database on steroids. The People hub is a way to keep track of people, presumably those who are somewhat less important than those who have their own tile on your Start screen. An example of the People hub is shown in Figure 4-3.

The People hub is your introduction to an important concept of Windows Phone 7: the hub. The hub is like a personal Web site on the Internet where all your sources of information are set up in a format that's easy to view on your Windows Phone. Part IV walks you through the steps of setting up your People hub.

After you've set it up, the panorama shows that there are three sections to the People hub:

- **Recent:** All the new contacts whom you've recently added to your People hub

- **All:** All your friends whom you've set up to be on your People hub

- **What's New:** All the latest messages and social network updates from any of your friends

You access the People hub from a tile on your Start screen. When you see a friend you want to communicate with on the People hub, you're shown all the options you have for communicating with that person.

Photos

The Photo hub helps you use the digital camera on your Windows Phone to its full potential.

Studies of cellphone users have found that we tend to snap a bunch of pictures on our phones the first month. After that, the photos sit on the phone (instead of being downloaded to our computers), and our picture-taking rate drops dramatically. When we upgrade to new phones, sometimes we lose the photos on our old phones, or only then do we take the time to download the images onto our home computers.

The Windows Phone is different. With the Photo hub (shown in Figure 4-4), you can integrate your camera images into your home photo library, as well as photo-sharing sites such as Flickr, with minimal effort. Plus, you can integrate these photos with your People hub and social networking sites (see the preceding section).

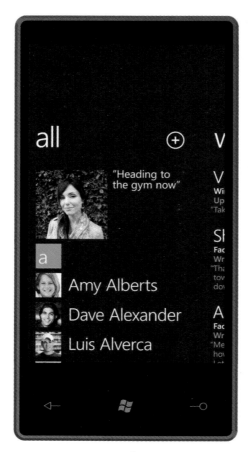

Courtesy of Microsoft Corporation

Figure 4-3: The People hub.

For more on how to use the Photo hub, turn to Chapter 11.

Music and video

Sure, your Windows Phone can take advantage of all that Zune has to offer (see "Multimedia," earlier in this chapter), but Windows Phone 7 also has the Music + Video hub (shown in Figure 4-5), which offers you more information than just what multimedia files are available on your phone. The Music + Video hub gives you rapid access to your new tracks and the tracks that you've been listening to most recently. There are also applications that can introduce you to music that is similar to what you've been playing.

Courtesy of Microsoft Corporation

Figure 4-4: The Photo hub takes your camera phone to a whole new level.

Games

In addition to the games that you can download from the Windows Phone Marketplace, the Windows Phone offers integration with the Microsoft Xbox LIVE Web site. This integration takes place through the Xbox LIVE hub (shown in Figure 4-6).

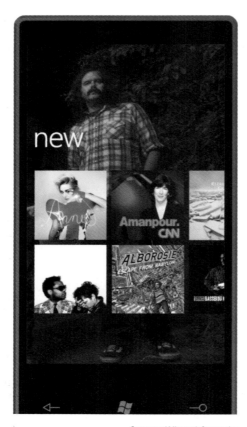

Courtesy of Microsoft Corporation

Figure 4-5: The Music + Video hub makes music and video listening easier.

The Xbox LIVE hub brings all your gaming assets together in one spot. You can access them whether you're on your Xbox console, a computer, or your Windows Phone.

The capabilities of the Xbox are such that no self-respecting Xbox fan should use any cellphone other than the Windows Phone. Sure, there may need to be a transition period while previous cellular phone carrier contracts expire, but after that, the gaming experience will be so well integrated among the different platforms that there will be no excuse for Xbox fans not to begin using a Windows Phone.

Figure 4-6: The Xbox LIVE hub takes your Xbox experience mobile.

Part VI of this book is for gamers. There, I give you all the information you need to set up different gaming experiences. Whether you prefer stand-alone games, multiplayer games, or Xbox-based games, you can set up your Windows Phone to get what you need.

Business and e-mail

Whether your company gives you a Windows Phone to use for work or you buy your Windows Phone yourself to improve your own productivity, the Windows Phone Office hub gives you the tools to keep on top of what happens in the office. A panorama view of the Office hub is shown in Figure 4-7.

The Office hub integrates the information on the Microsoft SharePoint system with the Microsoft Mobile Office applications on your Windows Phone. This allows you to access the latest version of any Microsoft Office file. In addition, you can access your office's Outlook e-mail system and integrate it with your e-mail on your phone.

These capabilities are truly unique to the Windows Phone. Part VII explores how to set up your Office hub.

Take a deep breath

You don't have to rush to implement every feature of your Windows Phone the very first day you get it. Instead, pick one hub that you want to set up before you tackle more — I recommend starting with the People hub. If you try to cram it all in on the first day, you'll turn what should be fun into drudgery.

No matter how you tackle the process of setting up your Windows Phone, it'll take some time. The good news is that you own the book that takes you through the process. You can do a chapter or two at a time.

Courtesy of Microsoft Corporation

Figure 4-7: The Office hub helps you stay on top of your work.

5

Included Applications: What's on Your Phone

In This Chapter

▶ Identifying all the apps on your Start screen

▶ Finding a list of all the apps on your phone

*Y*our Windows Phone comes with a variety of applications — tools that allow you to do all kinds of things, from managing your schedule to accessing the Internet, and more. In this chapter, I fill you in on the applications that are there from the get-go, and tell you where to find them.

You're not limited to the applications that came with your phone. For information on how to buy other applications for your phone, turn to Chapter 8.

Start Screen Apps: The Tip-Top Taps

Figure 5-1 shows you the full panorama of the Start screen. These are the tiles that you're most likely to tap first. When you first get the phone, all the tiles are applications. In Part IV and Chapter 21, I explain how you can set up your Start screen so that it displays *your* favorite contacts and applications.

Figure 5-1: The full panorama of the Start screen.

The applications accessible from the Start screen include

- **Internet Explorer:** The mobile version of the Web browser that's familiar to PC users
- **Office:** The mobile version of Microsoft Office
- **Clock:** A very simple application that — drum roll, please — presents the time
- **Calendar:** A calendar that allows you to store appointments and be alerted as their times approach
- **Calculator:** An algebraic calculator

These applications are the ones that Microsoft has determined to be the top priority for most Windows Phone users. Your cellular carrier may customize this screen by reprioritizing or adding an application that it sees as important.

In the following sections, I give you more information on each of the five apps on the Start screen.

Internet Explorer: It's all there

Internet Explorer, which comes standard with your Windows Phone, works almost identically to the version of Internet Explorer that's on your PC. You see many familiar toolbars, including Favorites and Search Engine.

The mobile version of Internet Explorer also includes tabs that allow you to open multiple Internet Explorer sessions simultaneously.

Chapter 6 goes into much more detail on using Internet Explorer on your Windows Phone, as well as the Web sites that you can access from your phone.

Office: Just like your PC

The Microsoft Office applications on the Windows Phone are designed to operate in many of the same ways as their PC counterparts. Unlike Microsoft Office for your PC, which has a list price of almost $400, Microsoft Office for Mobile comes with your Windows Phone at no additional charge. Here are the applications within the Microsoft Office for Mobile suite:

- **Microsoft Word:** A word processor for managing documents.
- **Microsoft Excel:** A spreadsheet application.
- **Microsoft PowerPoint:** An application for creating and viewing slideshow presentations.

 ✔ **Microsoft OneNote:** A tool for taking notes.

 ✔ **Microsoft SharePoint:** A collaboration tool that allows a team of individuals to maintain revisions of documents. Current files and earlier revisions are stored on a company's computer, but anyone with proper authorization can download a copy and make updates.

To launch an application, just tap the application's icon. The icons for the Microsoft Office for Mobile applications are shown in Figure 5-2.

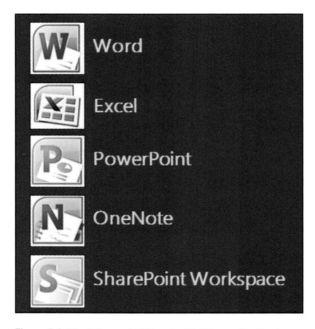

Figure 5-2: The Microsoft Office for Mobile application icons.

You can use the Office applications to view and create files on your phone, and those files will operate seamlessly with the PC versions. The main limitation is the screen size of your phone — accessing some of the commands isn't as easy on a small screen as it is on a larger one. Figure 5-3 shows an Excel document open on a Windows Phone. Even with the zoom-in and zoom-out features of your Windows Phone, creating a complex spreadsheet on your phone could be cumbersome. How far you take it is entirely up to you — the capabilities are all there.

Figure 5-3: What Excel looks like on your
Windows Phone.

Realistically, you'll want to share the files on your Windows Phone with your
PC at some point. Part VII explores the real-world ways of using these applications to work on home and business projects.

Clock: Anybody have the time?

In addition to showing the time, the Clock application also presents the current time in other world cities. The application has a default display but also
gives you options for *skins,* which present the present time using a variety of
formats (such as an analog clock face or a digital display).

You can change the Clock to your preference by tapping the ellipsis (. . .) icon at the bottom of the screen.

Calendar: Forget your appointment book

The Windows Phone has a stand-alone Calendar application in which you can set up appointments on your phone. Just tap the Calendar icon, and you see the daily calendar shown in Figure 5-4.

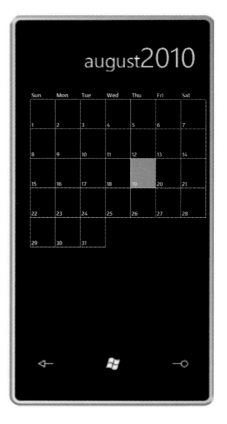

Figure 5-4: Daily and monthly calendars.

You can add an appointment by tapping on the plus sign on the screen. This brings up the New Appointment screen, shown in Figure 5-5. Enter the information into each field using the software keyboard, and — *voilà!* — you've scheduled an appointment on your phone.

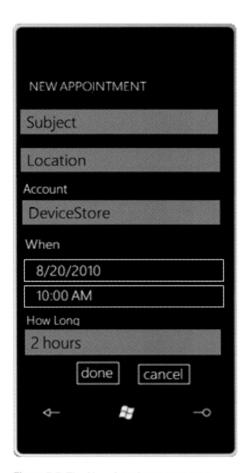

Figure 5-5: The New Appointment screen.

When the time of an appointment approaches, you'll get a pop-up message like the one shown in Figure 5-6. You can dismiss the notice or tap Snooze, to be reminded of the appointment later.

Figure 5-6: The screen alerting you to an approaching appointment.

If you look at the New Appointment screen (refer to Figure 5-5), you'll notice an Account text box. The only option shown in Figure 5-5 is DeviceStore, which means that the appointment is stored on your phone. But you also have the option to automatically update an electronic calendar — for example, your work e-mail system or a calendar on your home PC. To do this, you have to set up the appropriate connections. I cover setting up your personal calendar in Chapter 11 and your work calendar in Chapter 20.

Calculator: 1 + 1 = 2

The calculator (shown in Figure 5-7) is a straightforward algebraic calculator. And that's pretty much all there is to say about it.

Figure 5-7: The calculator.

Exploring More Applications on Your Phone

In the previous section, I cover all the applications that are on the Start screen. But by flicking the screen one page to the right, you get a complete list of the applications, utilities, and settings on your phone. Figure 5-8 shows the applications in panorama format. Even though this phone is new, the list of applications is extensive — and it'll grow as you add more applications.

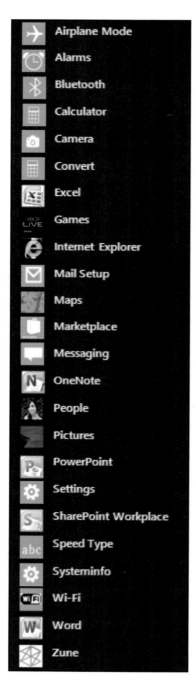

Figure 5-8: All the applications on your phone are just a flick away.

Applications

The applications accessible from the applications page include (but are not limited to) the following:

✓ **Alarms:** This application allows you to set a time for an alarm to go off. When you tab the Alarms icon, you get a screen with a list of saved alarm types (shown in Figure 5-9). This shows the current alarm settings, and each setting has its own name so that you can easily distinguish them. The Alarms settings include the time that the alarm will go off, what day of the week it will go off, and the sound it will make.

Figure 5-9: The Alarms Saved screen.

To create a new alarm, tap the plus sign, which brings up the New Alarm screen (shown in Figure 5-10). Here, you can set the options for the alarm.

Tap the Time box, and you're taken to the Choose Time screen (shown in Figure 5-11), where you can drag and flick the numbers to get to the time you want the alarm to go off. When you're set, tap the Done button to go back to the New Alarm screen.

Figure 5-10: The New Alarm screen.

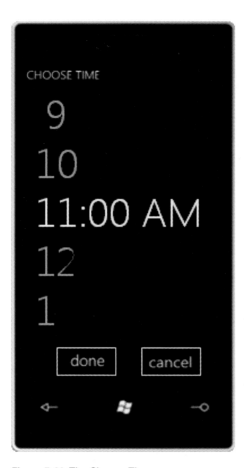

Figure 5-11: The Choose Time screen.

If you tap the Repeat box, you can set which days of the week you want the alarm to go off (see Figure 5-12). Tap Done, and you're taken back to the New Alarm screen.

Tap the Sound box, and you're taken to the Choose an Item screen (shown in Figure 5-13). Select the sound you want by tapping the name. The phone makes that sound when you tap it, so you can preview the sound and make sure it's what you want. Tap Done to go back to the New Alarm screen.

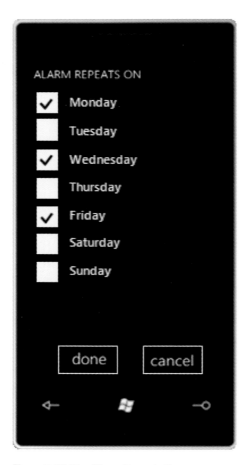

Figure 5-12: The Alarm Repeats On screen.

Finally, name this alarm to distinguish it from the other alarms that you've saved. To turn on the alarm, tap the toggle button to the right of the alarm name (refer to Figure 5-9).

- **Camera:** The Camera application allows you to take pictures. Chapters 10 and 11 explore what you can do with these pictures after you've taken them.

- **Convert:** The Convert application is a special-purpose calculator that converts units of measure (such as length, volume, and mass) into other formats. For example, the Convert application can convert meters to feet or pounds to kilograms.

✔ **Maps:** The Maps application takes you to Microsoft's Bing search engine. Chapter 6 explores how to get the most out of the search engine.

✔ **Marketplace:** Windows Phone Marketplace is the Microsoft site where you can get more applications for your phone. Turn to Chapter 8 for more on Marketplace.

✔ **Speed Type:** This is a Microsoft application that helps you become more comfortable with the software keyboard. It includes lessons you can complete to improve your typing on a Windows Phone.

Figure 5-13: The Choose an Item screen.

Utilities and settings

The utilities and settings accessible from the application page include

- **Airplane Mode:** Tapping this button brings you to a screen that has a toggle switch. Toggle it on and the cellular and Wi-Fi capabilities shut off. This allows you to use other capabilities on the phone (like listen to music or play games) while you're airborne, but you can't connect to the Internet.

- **Bluetooth:** The Bluetooth screen displays the Bluetooth devices that have been synched with your phone, and gives you the options of

  - Viewing currently synched devices

  - Synching a new Bluetooth device

  - Turning on or off the Bluetooth radio

- **Wi-Fi:** The Wi-Fi utility allows you to turn the Wi-Fi radio on or off.

Although Wi-Fi is very handy, you can save some battery life if you turn it off when you're in situation where you know that you can't access a Wi-Fi hotspot, such as in most cars. This saves the Wi-Fi radio in the phone from continuously and pointlessly searching.

Part III

Live on the Internet: Going Mobile

Seattle Art Museum

In this part . . .

The ability to access the Internet when you're away from your computer opens a new dimension of convenience, entertainment, and productivity. You don't want to have to lug around a laptop everywhere you go — and with a Windows Phone, you don't need to.

This part shows you how to get the most value out of the mobile Internet with as little hassle as possible. I tell you everything from how to access the mobile version of your favorite Web sites to how to buy new applications that run on your phone.

vodafone

6

You've Got the Whole (Web) World in Your Hands

*I*f you're like most people, one of the reasons you got a smartphone was because you wanted access to the Internet on your cellphone. You don't want to have to wait until you get back to your laptop or desktop to find the information you need online. You want to be able to access the Internet even when you're away from a Wi-Fi hotpot. And that's exactly what you can do with your Windows Phone. In this chapter, I show you how.

Browsing the Web on Your Phone: Internet Explorer

In Windows Phone 7, Microsoft includes a version of its popular Web browser, Internet Explorer. It isn't *exactly* the same as the Internet Explorer on your PC, though. Instead, the version of Internet Explorer that is running on your phone is designed to operate on a smaller screen.

To launch Internet Explorer on your Windows Phone, tap the Internet Explorer icon on the home page (shown in Figure 6-1).

Courtesy of Microsoft Corporation

Figure 6-1: Tap the Internet Explorer icon on the Start screen to get online.

As long as you're connected to the Internet (that is, either near a Wi-Fi hot-spot or in an area where you have cellular service), your home page appears. Your default home page could be blank, but most cellular carriers set their phones' home pages to their own Web sites or to a site selected by them.

Within Internet Explorer, there are four soft keys on the bottom of the screen:

- **The star with the plus sign:** Tapping this button adds the current Web site to your Favorites list.

- **The star:** Tapping this button brings up your Favorites list.

- **The tab button:** This button allows you to open up multiple Internet Explorer sessions.

- **The ellipsis button:** Tapping this button brings up more options to control Internet Explorer.

You can customize your home page by tapping the ellipsis and selecting Settings and then Home Page. This allows you to enter the default Internet Explorer home page that you want.

Your Favorites list

As convenient as it is to type with the keyboard, it's usually faster to store a Web address that you visit frequently in your Favorites. In this section, I tell you how to add a site to your Favorites list and view your existing Favorites. I also tell you how you can see your History list.

Adding to your Favorites

When you want to add a site to your Favorites, simply visit the site, and then tap the button with the star and the plus sign (shown in Figure 6-2). The Add Favorites screen (shown in Figure 6-3) appears. The name and URL of the site appear on this screen. You can change the name if you want. When you're satisfied, tap OK, and the phone adds that address to your Favorites folder.

Figure 6-2: The Add Favorites icon.

Figure 6-3: The Add Favorites screen.

Viewing your Favorites

To view what you have in your Favorites folder, tap the button with the star icon (shown in Figure 6-4), which brings you to the Favorites Center (shown in Figure 6-5). The Favorites list is in alphabetical order.

No one checks to see what you've called the Web sites in your Favorites list — you can call them whatever you want. For example, say one of your Favorites is Zygote Media Group (`www.zygote.com`), and you don't want to have to flick your way to the bottom of the list every time you want to access the Zygote site. Just add a number to the front of the name — for example, "1-Zygote" — and now Zygote is at the top of the list (displayed as "1-Zygote Media Group."

Figure 6-4: The Favorites icon.

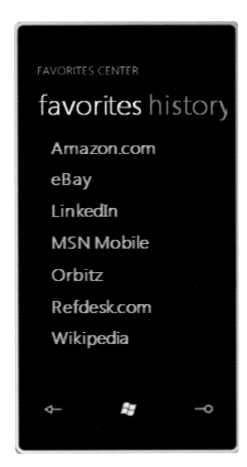

Figure 6-5: A typical Favorites list.

Your History

Just to the right of the Favorites list is your History list, a list of the Web sites you've viewed most recently. To see your History list, you can either tap the History label at the top of the screen or just pan to the right.

The History list is displayed with your most recent sites first. Accessing your History list is another way of getting to your favored sites, the ones you visit most often.

If you want to remove any of the entries from your History list, just tap the name and then drag it over to the garbage can icon at the bottom of the screen (shown in Figure 6-6).

Figure 6-6: Tap the garbage can icon to delete a site from your History list.

Tabs

Tabs were introduced in Internet Explorer in October 2006 with Internet Explorer 7. Before this, you could only view one session at a time, or you had to open multiple Internet Explorer sessions (which made for a complicated screen). With tabs, you can open multiple sessions by clicking New Tab on the tab line (as shown in Figure 6-7).

The version of Internet Explorer on your Windows Phone has the same capability, but it works a little differently from how it does on the PC. To navigate tabs on your phone, tap the Tab icon (shown in Figure 6-8).

The number you see on the Tab icon tells you how many tabs you have open.

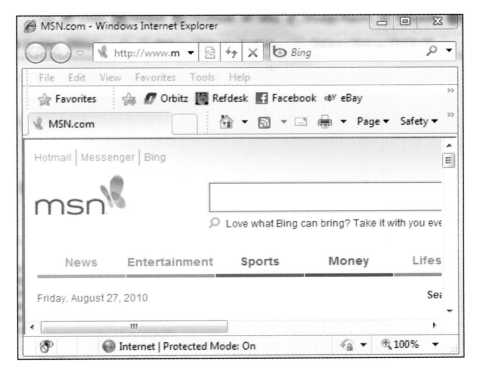

Figure 6-7: The tab line of the PC-based Internet Explorer.

Figure 6-8: The Tab icon.

After you tap the Tab icon, each tab presents as a miniature screen (as shown in Figure 6-9). Figure 6-9 shows three tabs that happen to be for Amazon.com, Google, and Engadget. To open a tab, tap it. To close a tab, tap the X within the circle; the other tabs will stay open.

Figure 6-9: The Tab screen.

To open a new tab, tap the plus sign toward the bottom of the screen. This brings up a blank screen. You can either type in a new URL or bring up a site from your Favorites list or History list.

More options

There is one more icon on the Internet Explorer page (refer to Figure 6-2). By tapping the ellipsis, you can bring up several options (shown in Figure 6-10):

Figure 6-10: The Options screen.

✔ **Forward:** The Forward command retraces your steps on an Internet Explorer session if you've used the hardware Back button. For example, maybe you've gone to the home page of a site and then tapped on a link to get the information you want — this is considered moving forward. Let's say that you want to move back to the home page — you press the Back button, which is a hardware key. Now, you're back on the home page again, and let's say you want to return to that link you advanced to moments ago — you can either tap the link again, or you can just tap Forward.

You may have noticed that moving forward with the Forward command requires two taps, while just tapping the link you used the first time is just a single tap. That's right: It's faster to just tap the link you used in the first place. You can leave the Forward command alone and only use it if you can't remember the path you used to get to where you were.

✔ **Share:** If you really like the Web site you're on, you can send the address to any contact you want. When you tap the Share command, you're asked who you want to send it to and how you want to send it (such as by e-mail or text message).

✔ **Find on Page:** Tapping the Find on Page command brings up a text box. You type in the text string of what you want the phone to search for on that page. If it finds the text you entered, your phone highlights it.

✔ **Pin to Start:** The Pin to Start command allows you to put that page as a tile on your Start screen. For example, if you get your news from *USA Today,* and you want to keep up with the news, you can pin the *USA Today* Web site (www.usatoday.com) as a tile on your Start screen. After it's pinned, that site will always be present when you turn on your phone, unless you remove it. The tile remains on your Start screen, even if you close Internet Explorer. Similarly, it is present as a tile when you power up your phone.

Before you start pinning your favorite Web sites to your home page, you may want to read about mobilized Web sites later in this chapter. For example, you may prefer to pin the mobile Web site for *USA Today* (http://m.usatoday.com) instead of the standard site.

✔ **Settings:** The Settings command allows you to adjust some settings for the operation of Internet Explorer.

Binging Your Way to the Information You Need: Mobile Bing Searches

When you open an Internet Explorer Mobile tab, you can use any search engine that you want (for example, Google or Yahoo!). Still, some functions — Web searches and map searches — work especially well when you use Microsoft's Bing search engine.

Web searches

Windows Phone is all about making Internet searches convenient. You can tap the Search button on the front of the phone and begin a search.

Actually, the Search button is sensitive to the context of what's on the screen. For example, if you're on a map search, it assumes you're searching for a location. If you're playing music, the Search button assumes you're searching for an artist or style of music. When you're at the Start screen, pressing the Search button does a general Internet search.

If you want to avoid worrying that the Search button limits itself to a location or music, you can always press the Start button first and then press the Search button.

The Internet search on your Windows Phone brings largely the same results that a Bing search on your PC brings, with two exceptions:

✔ **The Windows Phone screen is smaller.** The layouts on the screens are different. Most PCs are wider horizontally than vertically, but the Windows Phone is narrower horizontally when held upright (although you can turn your phone on its side to get the screen to operate with a wider horizontal screen). In addition, the *screen resolution* (the number of image pixels) is lower on the Windows Phone, primarily because the screen on the phone is smaller. To address these issues, Microsoft has spent a great deal of time making the presentation of information on Web search accommodate the smaller screen size with lower resolution.

The standard Bing home screen on a PC (shown in Figure 6-11) presents a different high-resolution image every day, overlaid with the search box. The image is always something dramatic. However, because it's high resolution, it takes more time to download than if the screen were optimized for the mobile environment.

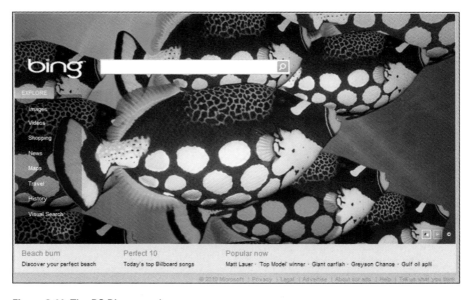

Figure 6-11: The PC Bing search screen.

Figure 6-12 shows the mobile version of Bing displayed on a Windows Phone. This is the screen that is set up to run on any mobile browser. As you can see, this is a minimalist screen, with only the Bing logo, a few configuration options, and the text box for the search.

Figure 6-12: The mobile Bing search screen.

Figure 6-13 shows the Windows Phone search engine. It's less complicated than the PC search, while more interesting than the minimalist mobile Bing search.

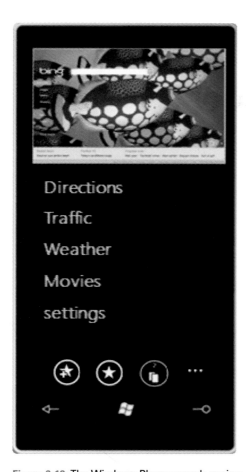

Figure 6-13: The Windows Phone search engine.

As you can see, the Windows Phone search engine has a low resolution version of the image from the full screen PC search screen.

✔ **Wherever you go, your phone follows you.** Bing searches from your PC are aware of the location of your PC, and adjust the responses to your location. This feature isn't intrusive and avoids giving you information about sites that have no relevance to your location. For example, you may want to find a store for some ice cream. If you're in, say, San Francisco, it does you little good to see a listing for Friendly's Ice Cream, because the closest store is 2,209 miles away in Defiance, Ohio. Friendly's is good, but not that good!

Windows Phones have a GPS receiver that tells the phone where you are. The search function on your phone takes your location into consideration when you enter data. For example, if you're from San Francisco, but you happen to be traveling in Ohio, you'd be made aware of the local Friendly's and could satisfy your craving for a Fribble shake.

Map searches: Getting there from here

The most direct way to use a map is to bring up the Maps application, which is accessible from the Application screen (see Chapter 5). You get there by starting at the Start screen and moving one screen to the right. Next, you flick down to the Maps icon (shown in Figure 6-14).

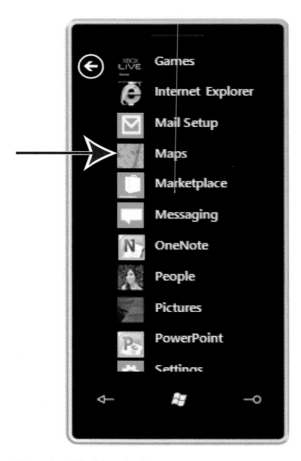

Figure 6-14: The Maps icon.

Tapping the Maps icon brings up a street map with your current location roughly centered. Figure 6-15 shows an example of a map when the phone user is in Seattle.

Figure 6-15: A map on a Windows Phone in Seattle.

The location of the user is at the center of the map. The resolution of the map of downtown Seattle starts at about 1 mile square. You can see other parts of the map by placing a finger on the map and dragging away from the part of the map that you want to see. That brings new sections of the map onto the screen.

You can turn the phone sideways to change the way the map is displayed. Depending on what you're looking for, this orientation may be easier.

You may be tempted to have the Maps application on your Start screen. Hold off on that one. The Maps application is integrated into many other applications and automatically launches when you tap on an address. (For more information, see "The automatic map," later in this chapter.)

Changing the scale of the map

The resolution of 1 square mile works under some circumstances to help you get oriented in an unfamiliar place. But sometimes it helps to zoom out to get a broader perspective or zoom in to help you find familiar landmarks, like a body of water or a major highway.

To get more real estate onto the screen, you use the pinch motion. This shrinks the size of the current map and brings in more of the map around where you're pinching. If you need more real estate on the screen, you can keep on pinching until you get more and more map. After you have your bearings, you can return to the original resolution by double-tapping on the screen.

On the other hand, the scale of 1 square mile may not be enough resolution. To get to see more landmarks, use the stretch motion to zoom in. The stretch motion expands the boundaries of the place you start on the screen. You can continue stretching and stretching until you get to the detail that you want.

When you get to a certain point, the Maps application automatically shifts from line drawings of a street map to a satellite image (as shown in Figure 6-16). The expectation is that, once you reach a certain point, what you're really seeking is not a street map, but some other landmark. Your Windows Phone takes care of this for you. You can return to the earlier scale by double-tapping on the screen.

The automatic map

You can open the Maps application like you open any other application. But, in practice, the most common way that you'll launch the Maps application is from *within* another application. Whenever the phone detects an address, it allows you to map it. For example, if you're in Defiance, Ohio, and you do a Web search on Friendly's Ice Cream, you would get the results show in Figure 6-17. The search turns up the address of the store, but also the Web site for the store and any other information that it senses may be of interest.

Figure 6-16: A satellite image from a Windows Phone map.

When you tap the address of the restaurant, your location and the location of the restaurant appears on a map (see Figure 6-18). This is much easier than having to write down the location where you're heading and tapping it into a text box in a Web browser.

The capability to automatically map an address works when you're doing a Web search or looking up the address of a friend from your contact database.

Figure 6-17: A Web search on a restaurant.

Accessing Web Sites, Mobile or Not

Earlier in this chapter, Figure 6-11 shows the Bing site for the PC, and Figure 6-12 shows the mobile version of this site. Bing is far from the only Web site to offer a mobile version of its site. Many sites — everything from Facebook to Flickr, Gmail to Wikipedia — offer mobile versions.

How do you get to the mobile Web sites? You don't have to worry about it! If there is a mobile version of the Web site you're visiting, Internet Explorer automatically brings it up.

When you search for a site with Bing, it places a phone icon next to the sites that are mobile optimized.

Figure 6-18: Directions to your search result.

When a site doesn't offer a mobile version (or when you just prefer to view the standard version of a particular site), you can stretch and pinch to find the information you need.

7

The Windows Live ID and What It Can Do for You

In This Chapter

▶ Identifying the importance of the Windows Live ID

▶ Determining whether you already have one

▶ Getting a Windows Live ID

To access the full capabilities of your Windows Phone, you need a Windows Live ID. Without a Windows Live ID, you just have a cellphone with a cool screen and a Web browser. With a Windows Live ID, you can load games, applications, music, videos, and photos onto your phone, as well as update your contacts on your PC, play multi-player games, and connect to your business files. Pretty powerful, isn't it?

I start this chapter by telling you all the things that Windows Live can do for you. Then I help you determine whether you already have a Windows Live ID. (Hey, you have a lot to keep track of — maybe you signed up and forgot.) Then I tell you how to get your very own Windows Live ID. Read on to unlock the powers of Windows Live.

Home   Profile   People   N.

..nday, May 24ᵗʰ

Bellevue, WA 63°
Private messages | Invitations
People you might know
Your calendar

What's new with Windows Live? Le

▢ **Your new profile** is all about you. Add more info, choose who can see it.
Edit your profile

▢ **Get free desktop programs**, including Messenger Gallery, Movie Maker, and more.
Learn more

'd **more people** to your network—you can eve
·∙r networks or address books.

Looking at the Benefits of Windows Live

Here are just some of the services that Microsoft offers with Windows Live as of this writing:

- ✔ **Microsoft Instant Messaging Service:** This is a popular PC service for instant messaging (IMing). It's comparable to AOL Instant Messenger (AIM) or Google Chat on a computer.

- ✔ **Windows Live Profile:** This service controls who and which PCs have permission to which files and services. Your Live Profile is your central repository for the privacy settings on all your Live services. If you want, you can ignore this site and just rely on the default settings. On the other hand, you can use the Live Profile to enable different levels of access and privacy for different people that you control.

- ✔ **Windows Live Calendar:** Live Calendar allows you to centralize and integrate all the information from your electronic calendars in a single place, while allowing them to retain their individual identities.

- ✔ **Windows Live Contacts:** Live Contacts allows you to centralize and integrate all the information from your electronic contact databases into a single master database.

- ✔ **Windows Live SkyDrive:** SkyDrive allows you to store large amounts of files on a computer hard drive that's connected remotely from your phone or PC. These files can be anything, including music, Office files, photos, games, and applications. The files are always available and are secure. The connection is slower than it would be if it were on a drive connected directly to your PC.

- ✔ **Windows Live Writer:** Live Writer is intended to help you prepare blogs. It's sort of like a simplified version of Microsoft Office, with the ability to integrate text and images.

- ✔ **Windows Movie Maker:** This site offers you tools for editing video files.

- ✔ **Windows Photo Gallery:** This service is comparable to Flickr. You can upload photos, organize them in albums, and put descriptive data on each photo.

- ✔ **Xbox LIVE:** Xbox LIVE allows you to access Xbox games and play against other people.

- ✔ **Zune:** This is the music and video service that works with Zune players and with computers that have downloaded the Zune application.

Microsoft adds, removes, and renames services from time to time, so don't think of this list as carved in stone.

The Windows Live ID is the key to accessing these services on your PC and/or on your phone. These applications and services are the basis for making your Windows Phone a tool to access all the information you use in your life and work. The advantage for you is that you create information once, and it's automatically shared with your phone, your work PC, your personal PC, and any PC that you may borrow.

Determining whether You Have a Windows Live ID

You may already have a Windows Live ID. There are a number of situations in which this could be the case:

- ✔ You have an e-mail account from Microsoft, with an ending of `msn.com`, `hotmail.com`, or `live.com`

- ✔ You have an earlier version of Windows Phone, formerly known as Windows Mobile, and have access to the Windows Phone Marketplace.

- ✔ You signed up for one of the following services from Microsoft:
  - Microsoft Instant Messaging Service
  - Windows Live Profile
  - Windows Live Calendar
  - Windows Live Contacts
  - Windows Live Essentials
  - Windows Live SkyDrive
  - Windows Live Writer
  - Windows Movie Maker
  - Windows Photo Gallery
  - Xbox LIVE Service
  - Zune

- ✔ You signed up for an earlier version of the Windows Live ID, when it was called Microsoft Wallet, Microsoft Passport, or .NET Passport.

Microsoft has a habit of renaming services when those services don't live up to internal expectations. It's supposed to send a signal that the new version is "new and improved." If you're a user of that service, you may just find it annoying or confusing.

To find out if you already have a Windows Live ID, go to `http://login.live.com`, enter your e-mail address, and take a stab at your password. If it works, you'll see the screen shown in Figure 7-1. If it doesn't recognize your password, you'll get the screen shown in Figure 7-2; follow the instructions for resetting your password. Finally, if you haven't set up that e-mail address to be a Windows Live ID, you'll see a message that says

```
The Windows Live ID is incorrect. Please try again.
```

No problem. Just continue on to the next section of this chapter.

Figure 7-1: The Windows Live home page.

Figure 7-2: The Windows Live ID password reset page.

Signing Up for a Windows Live ID

When you're signing up for a Windows Live ID, the first decision you need to make is whether to use an existing e-mail account as your Live ID or to create a new e-mail account. There's no advantage in terms of convenience or access to services in using a Microsoft e-mail address versus any other e-mail address.

Open Sesame: Your Windows Live ID password

If your e-mail address is from Microsoft, your password for e-mail is *always* your password for your Windows Live ID. If you change your password for your e-mail account, you're also changing the password for your Windows Live ID, and vice versa.

If your e-mail is not from Microsoft, your password for your Windows Live ID is your choice. You can use the same password you use for your e-mail, or you can use something different.

When you initially choose your Windows Live ID password (or when you change your password after you've already signed up), an onscreen indicator tells you whether it considers the password to be weak, medium, or strong. Your password must be at least six characters in length. It'll be stronger if you use a mix of uppercase and lowercase letters, special characters, and numbers.

Remember: If you write down the password on a sticky note and post it on your monitor, you defeat the purpose of a strong password. Research has shown that the greatest number of security breaches come from human error, like using sticky notes to store passwords, and not from hackers.

If you have a personal e-mail account that you plan to keep for a while, go ahead and use that personal e-mail address as your Live ID. On the other hand, if you need a new personal e-mail account for some reason, now is a good time to create a new one.

If you've been relying on your work e-mail address as your only e-mail, you probably want to sign up for a personal e-mail address. First, you may not stay at that company forever, and it's convenient to have an e-mail address that sticks with you wherever you go. Plus, even if your employer allows you to use your work e-mail address for personal e-mails, your employer has the right to read your work e-mail. It's just a good idea to keep work and personal e-mails separate, for obvious reasons.

Knowing what information you need to provide

Regardless of whether you're going to use an existing e-mail address or get a new one, you'll need to provide the following information:

- ✔ Your first and last name
- ✔ Your gender
- ✔ Your birth year
- ✔ A Windows Live ID password (see the nearby sidebar, "Your Windows Live ID password")
- ✔ Your response to an acknowledgment of the Microsoft terms

Some people feel that even these basic questions are intrusive. To retain a sense of anonymity, you may be tempted to put in a fictional name and location. If you claim that you're Santa Claus and live in North Pole, Alaska, get ready: You'll be welcomed with "Hi, Santa!" when you log in, and you'll be directed to something like Mama C's Moose Creek Kitchen when you look for restaurants in your local area. It's just easier to be honest about who you are and where you live.

Jumping through the hoops

To sign up for your Windows Live ID, go to `http://login.live.com` (shown in Figure 7-3). Click the Sign Up for an Account link, and you're taken to a page that gives you a choice of using an existing e-mail account or creating a new one (see Figure 7-4).

Figure 7-3: The Windows Live sign-in screen.

If you choose to use an existing e-mail account, the page will look like the one shown in Figure 7-5. If you want to create a new e-mail account, the page will look like the one shown in Figure 7-6.

Figure 7-4: Choose whether you want to create a new e-mail address or use an existing one.

Figure 7-5: You'll see this if you use an existing e-mail account.

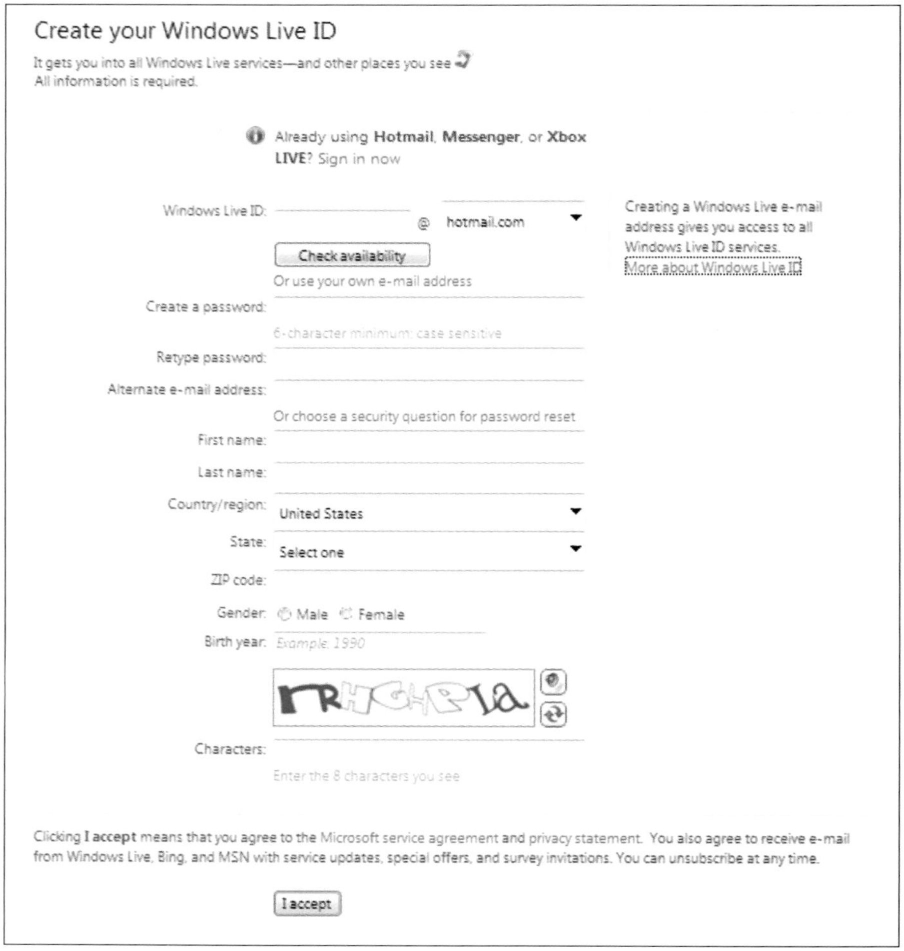

Figure 7-6: You'll see this if you want to create a new e-mail account.

Acknowledging your new Windows Live ID

After you create a Windows Live ID and password, enter your personal data, and accept the Microsoft terms, Microsoft sends you an e-mail letting you know that a request has been made to create a Windows Live ID. Open that e-mail and click the link to acknowledge your Windows Live ID.

Congratulations! You now have a Windows Live ID with all the rights and privileges thereof.

Coming up with a new e-mail address

If you aren't using an existing e-mail account as your Windows Live ID, you'll want to come up with a few options for e-mail addresses, unless the name you want isn't very common.

Keep in mind the following tips:

✓ **The address can contain only letters, numbers, periods (.), hyphens (-), or underscores (_).** The letters are not case sensitive, so if you prefer the look of SantaClaus to santaclaus, use capital letters where you want.

✓ **Consider adding prefixes or suffixes to your name.** For example, MrSantaClausPhD or MsToothFairyEsq may be available, whereas just plain SantaClaus and ToothFairy may be taken.

✓ **Try adding numbers to the end of your name.** For example, you may want to use your birth year, your lucky number, or your street address.

When you're signing up for a new e-mail address as part of the Windows Live ID registration process, you'll be offered suggestions that are close to what you've requested if your first choice is already taken. For example, if you want the address Windows_Phone_7@hotmail.com, but that address is already taken, you'll be offered similar names, such as Windows_Phone_8@hotmail.com or Windows.p.h.o.n.e@live.com. If Windows_Phone_7@live.com were available, you would be given that as an option.

Introducing the Windows Phone Marketplace

*O*ne of the things that makes smartphones, like the phones based on Windows Phone 7, different from regular cellphones is that you can download better applications than what come standard on the phone.

Most traditional cellphones come with a few simple games and basic applications that let you manage the numbers that you've called or that have called you. Smartphones usually come with better games and applications. For example, you get a more sophisticated contact manager, an application that can play digital music (MP3s), basic maps, and texting tools.

You can get even better applications and games for phones based on Windows Phone 7. Numerous applications are available for your Windows Phone — and that number will grow over time.

So, where do you get all these wonderful applications? The only place to get apps for your phone is at the Windows Phone Marketplace. You may be happy with the applications that came with your Windows Phone, but look into the Windows Phone Marketplace, and you'll find apps you suddenly won't be able to live without.

In this chapter, I introduce you to the Windows Phone Marketplace and give you a taste of what you find there. For information on how to buy and download apps, turn to the next chapter.

Windows Phone Marketplace: The Mall for Your Phone

Windows Phone Marketplace is set up and run by Microsoft, primarily for the benefit of people with Windows Phones. Adding an application to your phone is similar to adding software to your PC. In both cases, a new application (or new software) makes you more productive, adds to your convenience, and entertains you for hours on end. Not a bad deal.

There are some important differences, however, between installing software on a PC and getting an application on a cellphone:

- **Smartphone applications need to be more stable than computer software because of their greater potential for harm.** If you buy an application for your PC and find that it's unstable (for example, it causes your PC to crash), you'll be upset. If you were to acquire an unstable application for your phone, you could run up a huge phone bill or even take down the regional cellphone network. Can you hear me now?

- **With a smartphone, you're limited in terms of where you can buy new apps.** You can get software for your computer at retail stores or off the Internet, but you can get applications for your Windows Phone only from the Windows Phone Marketplace.

- **The validity of your smartphone software is checked (in the background) each time you use it.** Many PC applications occasionally check for updates, but applications on your Windows Phone are authorized each time you open them. The good news for you is that, if a newer version of the app is available, Windows Phone tells you that you may want, or need, to upgrade.

- **There are multiple smartphone platforms.** These days, it's safe to assume that computer software runs on a PC or a Mac or both. On the other hand, there are various smartphone platforms out there, and different versions within a given platform are not always compatible. Marketplace ensures that the application you're buying will work with your version of the Windows Phone.

Microsoft has set up the Windows Phone Marketplace to address some of these issues. Specifically, in the Windows Phone Marketplace, you get

✔ **Free trial periods:** Application developers can choose to offer free trial periods on their apps (or not to offer free trial periods), but Microsoft is encouraging authors of apps sold through the Marketplace to offer a free trial so that users can get a taste of an application without making a full commitment to buy.

✔ **Money-back guarantees:** If you don't like the app, you can return it (actually disable it) within seven days and get your money back.

How to Get to the Marketplace

There are two ways to get to the Marketplace: through your Windows Phone's Marketplace application, or through the Internet. I cover both of these methods in this section.

Through the Marketplace app on your Windows Phone

The easiest way to access the Marketplace is through the Marketplace application on your Windows Phone. You access this by going to the application list just to the right of the Start screen. Flick down to Marketplace and tap to open it. This takes you to the Marketplace panorama (shown in Figure 8-1).

Through the Internet

If you prefer, you can also access the Marketplace using a Web browser, either on your phone or on your computer. The Web address for Windows Phone Marketplace is `http://marketplace.windowsphone.com`. When you visit the site, you'll see a screen that looks like Figure 8-2.

As new applications become available, the highlighted applications will change, and the home page will change from one day to the next — but the categories will be consistent over time. These categories are

✔ **Showcase:** Showcase highlights some valuable application or game that you may not otherwise come across. This is the first screen that you'll see (the left-most screen on the panorama).

✔ **Most Popular:** As the name implies, these are the most-downloaded applications. Popularity is a good initial indication that the application is worth considering.

Figure 8-1: The Marketplace panorama on a Windows Phone.

✓ **What's New:** These are new applications. If you're already familiar with what's available in the Marketplace, this category helps you see what's changed.

✓ **Categories:** Marketplace labels each application to make it easier for you to find it in the store. The Windows Phone Marketplace is the one site for all your Windows Phone–related purchases, including applications, games, and music.

You can access the Marketplace without signing in, and you can check out all the applications and games that are available on the site. However, you'll have to sign in with your Windows Live ID (see Chapter 7) to determine which applications and games will work on your particular phone or to buy an application.

The applications that run on Windows Mobile, which Microsoft has renamed Windows Phone Classic, will not run on Windows Phone 7, just as the applications for the iPhone will not run on Windows Phone 7.

The Sign In button is in the upper-right corner of the home page (refer to Figure 8-2). When you click this link, you're taken to the screen shown in Figure 8-3. Here, you have to supply your Windows Live ID. (If you're already signed in, you'll be taken immediately to all the available applications.)

Figure 8-2: The Windows Phone Marketplace home page.

What's Available: Window Shopping

When you head to the local mall with a credit card but without a plan, you're asking for trouble. Anything and everything that tickles your fancy is fair game. Similarly, before you head to the Windows Phone Marketplace, it helps if you have a sense what you're looking for, so you don't spend more than you intended.

Throughout this book, I use the term *applications* to refer to games or other kinds of applications. Some purists make a distinction between applications and games. The thing is, from the perspective of a phone user, they're the same. You download an application and use it, either for fun or to be more productive.

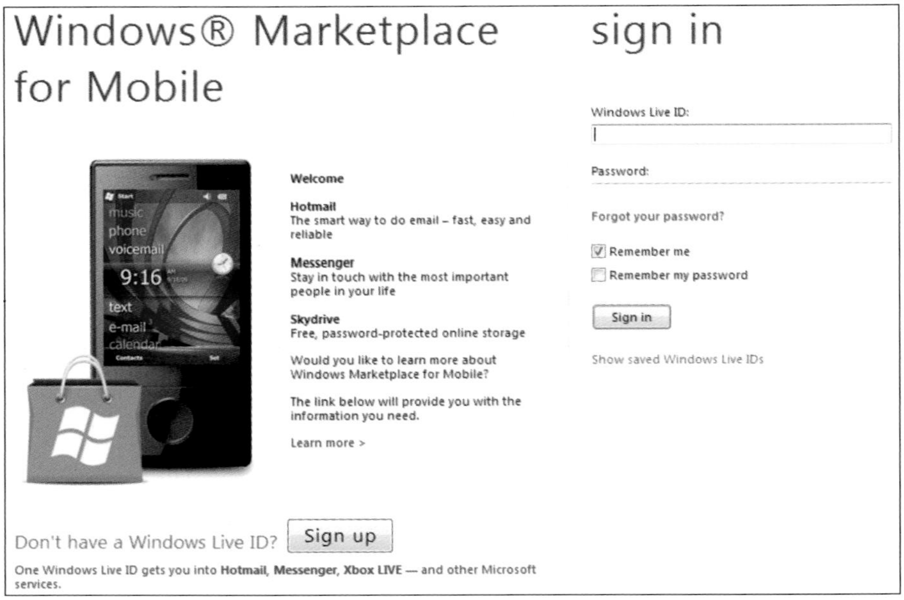

Courtesy of Microsoft Corporation

Figure 8-3: The Windows Marketplace sign-in page.

Applications for your Windows Phone fall into two main categories — games and everything else:

- **Games:** Your Windows Phone takes interactive gaming to a new level. Games on your Windows Phone fall into two categories:

  - Stand-alone games that are downloaded and run locally on your phone

  - Web-based games that are accessed through the Xbox LIVE Web site, including single- and multi-player games (see Chapter 19)

  Accessing games on Xbox LIVE is a very exciting and unique capability within Windows Phone devices.

  The Marketplace lets you access both kinds of games.

- **Everything else:** The list of all the applications that you can download to your phone is long, but they fall into the following categories:

  - **Books:** You can download books to your smartphone, just as you can to an Amazon Kindle or Sony Reader. The screen on your Windows Phone is smaller and the selection of books is tiny.

However, you can get some classics for very little money or even free.

- **Business Center:** These applications — such as business calculators and business-trip expense-tracking tools — make you more productive at work.

- **Communication:** Yes, the Windows Phone comes with many communications applications. But these apps in the Marketplace enhance what comes with the phone. For example, you find tools that automatically send a message if you're running late to a meeting or that text you if your kids leave a defined area.

- **Reference:** These apps include a range of reference books, such as dictionaries and translation guides. Think of this like the reference section of your local library and bookstore.

- **Entertainment:** These apps aren't games, but they're still fun. Here you find apps having to do with trivia, horoscopes, and frivolous noise-making apps.

- **Lifestyle:** This category is a catch-all for applications that involve health and fitness, recreation, photography, and shopping.

- **Maps & Search:** Many applications tell you where you are and where you want to go. Some are updated with current conditions, while others are based upon static maps that use typical travel times.

- **Music & Video:** The Windows Phone comes with the Zune service, which offers access to music and video, but you may prefer offerings that are set up differently or have a selection of music that isn't currently available on Zune.

- **News & Weather:** You find a variety of apps that allow you to drill down into getting just the news or weather that is more relevant to you.

- **Productivity:** These apps are for money management (like a tip calculator), voice recording (like a stand-alone voice recorder), and time management (for example, an electronic to-do list).

- **Travel:** These apps are useful for traveling, such as currency converters, translations, and travel guides.

9

Buying and Installing Applications

*I*n Chapter 8, I tell you what the Windows Phone Marketplace is, how to access it, and what it offers you. In this chapter, I look at the mechanics and logistics of acquiring new applications for your phone, as well as how to get rid of the apps you no longer want (and maybe even get your money back).

Setting Your Marketplace Preferences

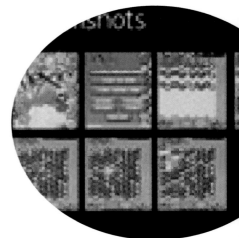

You don't have a ton of choices for Marketplace settings, but a couple of them are key. You access them from the Account Settings page (shown in Figure 9-1) on your PC. To get here, log in to Windows Phone Marketplace (see Chapter 8), and click Account Settings. (Pretty simple, huh?)

Figure 9-1: The Account Settings page in Windows Phone Marketplace.

Your payment information

To pay for your Marketplace purchases, you can either use a credit card or have them billed to your cellphone account through your cellular carrier.

Being billed by your cellular carrier is more convenient if your phone bill is paid by someone else, like another family member or your employer, or if you don't have or like to use credit cards.

Your wireless carrier may not allow you to have your Marketplace purchases billed to your cellphone account. If this option is important to you, check with the carrier before you sign a contract.

Your phone type

You tell Marketplace your phone type by clicking on the Device link and selecting Windows Phone 7. Then it shows you only the applications that your phone can use. (Not every application works on every type of phone.) This service is valuable — after all, why waste your time looking at apps you can't use?

You can enter up to five phones per Windows Live ID, which is convenient if you own or are responsible for multiple phones. If you do have multiple phones, however, make sure that the application you're downloading for a particular phone works on that phone. The application description makes this clear.

Your phone type is only relevant when you're browsing the Windows Phone Marketplace from your PC. If you're on your phone, you see only the applications that work on your phone.

Buying and Installing an Application from Your Phone

To buy and install an app on your Windows Phone, push the Start button to get to the Start screen. Then drag the screen so you move right to the alphabetical list of applications, flick down until you see the Marketplace application, and tap on the Marketplace icon. (Refer to Chapter 8 if you want more information.)

Earlier Windows Phone versions, which are called Windows Mobile, allow you to download an application to your PC and then connect your phone to your PC via a cable, transferring the app to your phone that way. This process is called *side-loading.* The Windows Phone requires you to download *over the air* (wirelessly), which is actually more convenient because it requires only one step. But some people still prefer the sense of control of first downloading to their PCs. Plus, it avoids any usage charges for mobile data service. Microsoft may add side-loading to the Windows Phone in the future.

Now you're ready to buy and download an app. Here's how:

1. **Tap on the application you want.**

   The description of the application appears (see Figure 9-2).

   The description page includes

   - **Title:** The formal title of the application
   - **Ratings summary:** A five-point ranking of the application by current users
   - **The price**
   - **Description:** A few sentences summarizing the application
   - **Features:** Highlights of the product
   - **Application requirements:** Any special considerations that may be useful to know before acquiring the application
   - **Release date**
   - **Version**
   - **Company contact information**
   - **Ratings and reviews**
   - **Screenshot:** A representative image of the application in use

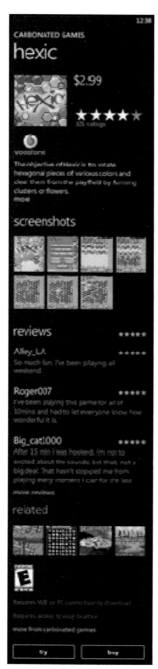

Courtesy of Microsoft Corporation

Figure 9-2: A description of an application.

2. **Tap the Buy button.**

   The Download Complete page (shown in Figure 9-3) appears.

   If you want to change your billing preferences for this transaction, tap the Change Billing Option link.

3. **Tap the Confirm button to confirm that you want to purchase the app.**

   The application download begins.

If the download is interrupted because, say, your phone battery dies or you leave your coverage area, the download picks up again where it left off as soon as you have a connection again. You don't have to do anything to make this happen.

Figure 9-3: The Download Complete page.

When the download process is over, a message appears on the screen.

4. **Start using the application.**

The phone adds the application to your application list. To launch it, push the Start button to return to the Start screen, drag to the screen of the alphabetical list of applications, flick down until you see the application you just bought, tap the application icon, and have fun!

Getting Application Updates

Sometimes an application you own is updated by the developer. The update may fix a bug or add new features. Whenever this happens, the manufacturer will let you know of the update. It may choose to send you an e-mail or have a message pop-up on your screen.

With the way things are set up on your phone, Microsoft and the software developer know who you are, so they can let you know if there is an update in the most effective or least intrusive way.

Let's say that it is an urgent bug fix that could cause problems if you do not upgrade. They would send you a pop-up message. If they have an upgrade that you might enjoy, they would send message to you. Depending on the software manufacturer, you may be able to tell them your preference for finding out about new information.

Preventing disappointment in the first place

Besides the full refund, there are a few options that Microsoft supports in an effort to prevent you from being disappointed. The possible options that an application developer can choose include the following:

- ✔ **You buy the application, but you aren't charged until you've had it for a week.** As long as you uninstall the app within a week of your first time having installed it, you aren't charged.

- ✔ **The application comes with a counter that lets you use it a fixed number of times (say, seven times), before it tells you that your** account will be charged if you continue using it.

- ✔ **A simple version of the application is free on Marketplace, but a better version is for sale.** The idea here is that you try out the free version, and if you like it enough, you buy the pay version. Of course, even if you don't like the pay version, you can still get a refund if you uninstall within a week.

Warning: Be sure to read the app description in the Marketplace to determine which of these options the developer is offering.

Why is Microsoft checking my applications?

You may find the fact that Microsoft is checking the software on your phone to be a little creepy or intrusive. However, most smartphones do this in some form. Why? Well, theoretically, it's possible for malware to get control of a smartphone and make it violate laws or regulations from the Federal Communications Commission (FCC). Microsoft and all its competitors test mobile software against this kind of behavior. This malware may be either intentional (like a computer virus) or just careless programming.

There are some benefits to Microsoft's aggressive checking. First, there is much less of a chance that your phone will become unresponsive during an emergency, send your personal data to an identify thief, or give your location to a stalker. Plus, the system can automatically send bug fixes and some upgrades to your software when they're available.

Getting Rid of an App — And Maybe Even Getting Your Money Back

It happens. You've downloaded an app, sure that it would be the answer to all the time you spend on the bus or train or plane, only to find that really, the app isn't as cool as you thought it would be. Here's how to get rid of it:

1. **Open the Marketplace application (see Chapter 8).**

2. **Tap the ellipsis.**

   The options for Marketplace appear at the bottom of the screen.

3. **Tap the Purchase History button.**

   All the applications you've purchased are listed. Adjacent to each tile is the date you downloaded the application and an option to uninstall.

4. **Tap the Uninstall button next to the application.**

   A screen appears, asking you to confirm that you do, indeed, want that application to go away.

5. **Tap the Confirm button.**

   The application is gone.

If you bought the app seven days ago (or less), you'll get a refund from Microsoft — either to the credit card you used to pay for the app, or to your cellphone bill, if that's how you paid.

Microsoft has heavily and enthusiastically promoted the seven-day return period. At the same time, such policies can disappear with minimal fanfare. If the seven-day return policy is in effect when you buy the software, the Windows Phone Marketplace will certainly honor it. If you don't see it for some reason, it may have been withdrawn.

Part IV
Connecting with the People You Care About

The 5th Wave   By Rich Tennant

"Your mail program looks fine. I don't know why you're not receiving any personal e-mails. Have you explored the possibility that you may not have any friends?"

august 2010

U ## In this part . . .

our phone is largely about staying connected with the people who are most important to you. A regular cellphone is about talking to and texting with these people. Your Windows Phone is about much, much more. You can connect with them through e-mail, social networks, contact databases . . . and, oh yeah, through phone calls and text messages, too. In this part, I show you how.

...

Add to Favorites

Delete

Share to Windows Live

Share to...

Shai Bassli

FACEBOOK, WINDOWS LIVE

what's new pro

This weather is driving me nuts!

2 hours ago

10

A Shared Picture Is Worth a Million Words

In This Chapter

▶ Taking a picture on your phone

▶ Organizing your pictures on your phone

▶ Sharing your pictures with friends and family

*1*f you are like many cellphone users, you love that you can take photographs with your cellphone. You probably carry your phone a lot more places than you carry your camera, so you never again have to miss a great photograph because you left your camera at home.

In this chapter, I tell you how to take a photograph, how to organize the photos you've already taken, and how to share your photos with friends and family.

Say Cheese! Taking a Picture with Your Windows Phone

Before you can take a picture, you have to open the Camera app. The easiest way to open the Camera app is simply to press the dedicated Camera button. When you press the Camera button, the Camera app launches.

When the Camera app is open, you're ready to take a picture. And how do you do that? Press the Camera button again. Easy as pie.

Sorting the Images on Your Phone

When you snap a picture, it's immediately stored as a file on your phone and handed over to the Pictures app for care and handling.

The Camera application and the Pictures application are closely related but are two separate apps.

Microsoft has put a great deal of thinking into the Pictures app and how to make it more convenient for you. In this section, I walk you through your sorting options.

A quick tour through the Pictures app

The images stored on your phone are accessible through the Pictures app, which has its own tile on the Start screen (see Figure 10-1).

For skeptics only

If you had a cameraphone in the past, you may be thinking, "What's the big deal? Cameraphones aren't worth the megapixels they're made of." It's true: In the past, many cameraphones weren't quite as good as cameras were, but the good news is, Microsoft has addressed these issues with Windows Phone 7. Here's how:

✔ **Resolution:** The resolution on most cameraphones is lower than what you typically get on a digital camera. But Microsoft has required that every Windows Phone have a camera with *at least* 5 megapixels. (The actual resolution of your phone depends upon the manufacturer.) A 5-megapixel photograph produces a 4-x-6-inch print that is indistinguishable from what you could produce with a film camera.

✔ **Photo transfer:** With most cameraphones, the photos are hard to move from the camera to a computer. With the Windows Phone, you can quickly and easily send an image, or a bunch of images, anywhere you want, wirelessly.

✔ **Screen resolution:** In practice, many cameraphone users just end up showing their pictures to friends right on their phones. Many cameraphone screens, however, don't have very good resolution, which means your images don't look so hot when you want to show them off to your friends. The good news is, the Windows Phone has a bright, higher-resolution screen. Photos look really good on the screen of a Windows Phone.

✔ **Organization:** Most cameraphones don't offer much in the way of organization tools. Your images are all just there on your phone, without any structure. But the Windows Phone has a Photo app that makes organizations of your photos as easy as possible.

Plus, your Windows Phone embeds *metadata* in each image. Metadata is the information about a digital file (in this case, a picture), including the date the picture was taken, which is a help when organizing your files.

Courtesy of Microsoft Corporation

Figure 10-1: The Pictures tile on the Start screen.

You can set any picture that you like to be on the tile image. In Figure 10-2, you see a picture of a boy in a canoe. Sure, that boy's mother thinks he's adorable, but if you want to get rid of canoe boy, feel free. (See the next section for instructions on how to do that.)

Tapping on the Pictures tile brings up the Pictures app. The home page (shown in Figure 10-2) gives you three choices:

✓ **Albums:** When you click Albums, you're taken to all the photo albums you've organized on your phone. The Album option allows you to group together a bunch of individual photos. For example, you might create an album called "Family Vacation," another album called "Prom Pictures," and a third album called "Baby Pictures." You select which pictures go into an album. (For instructions on creating a new album, see the next section.)

Courtesy of Microsoft Corporation

Figure 10-2: The home page for the Pictures app.

✔ **All:** When you click All, you're taken to all the photos you have on your phone, sorted by date (see Figure 10-3).

✔ **Favorites:** When you click Favorites, you're taken to your favorite photos. Favorites is essentially an album that you've built by marking particular photos as your favorites.

By default, Favorites has a tile on your Start screen, so you're always only a press and a tap away from your favorite pictures: Press the Start button and then tap the Favorites tile.

Figure 10-3: The "All" Category in the Photo Application

Whether you're in the Albums category, the All category, or the Favorites category, you can open a picture by tapping on it. The picture fills the screen, as shown in Figure 10-4.

Your sorting options

Organizing your photos into albums is important. After you've been taking photos for a while, the job of organizing gets more difficult. You can't remember if that picture of Johnny was from spring break or Easter. Start putting your pictures in albums sooner rather than later!

Figure 10-4: When you want to look at a particular picture, it fills the screen.

To start sorting photos, all you have to do is bring up a picture by tapping it (see the preceding section). When you're looking at the picture (refer to Figure 10-4), tap the picture, and a menu of options appears (see Figure 10-5).

A single tap on the photo brings up the sorting menu. A double-tap on the photo zooms in on the photo instead. If you get the wrong result, it means that you tapped twice instead of once. You can just tap once on the picture, even when zoomed in, and you'll get the sorting menu.

Figure 10-5: Your sorting options.

Here are the sorting options:

- **Add to Favorites:** Moves the photo to your Favorites album.
- **Delete:** Permanently deletes the photo from your phone.
- **Share to Windows Live:** See the next section.
- **Share To:** Allows you to send the photo via e-mail or text message.
- **Assign to Contact:** Allows you to sort pictures as a part of the People hub. For more on this, turn to Chapter 12.

✔ **Use as Wallpaper:** Sets this image so that it appears on the Photo tile on your Start screen.

✔ **View Album:** Takes you back to the album where the photo came from — if you've just taken the photo, it's likely in the All category.

To create a new album, follow these steps:

1. **Starting from the Pictures app home page (refer to Figure 10-2), tap the Albums link.**

   The Albums screen appears, presenting a list of tiles that represent the existing albums (see Figure 10-6).

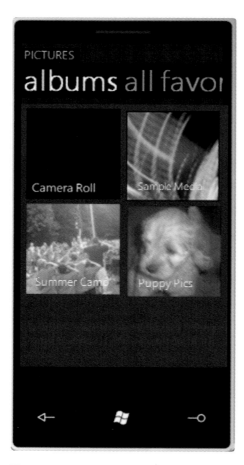

Figure 10-6: The Albums screen on the Photos Application.

2. **Tap the plus sign at the bottom of the screen.**

3. **Name the album.**

4. **Add photos from your phone.**

Sharing Your Photos with Windows Live

Windows Live Photo Gallery is a Web site where people can post pictures and organize them in albums.

It is possible to set up the permissions from your phone, but it's easier to do so from your PC.

You can choose who gets to see your images by setting up permissions. The service is free and available to anyone with a Windows Live ID (see Chapter 7). Along the top of the Windows Live home page (www.windowslive.com), you see the Web-based applications that are a part of Windows Live, including Photos (see Figure 10-7). When you click this link, you're taken to the Windows Live Photo Gallery home page, shown in Figure 10-8.

Figure 10-7: The Photos link on the Windows Live home page.

Figure 10-8: The Windows Live Photo Gallery home page.

On the Windows Live Photo Gallery home page, you see a Create Album link. When you click this link, the screen in Figure 10-9 appears. Here, you enter

- ✔ **The album name:** Name the album something that's meaningful to you and whoever you plan to share the album with. You may know that 2011-03-SB means "Spring Break 2011," but not everyone looking at your albums will know that, so be as clear as you can be.

- ✔ **Who you want to share the album with:** The Share With drop-down menu allows you to define who can see the pictures:

    - • **Everyone (Public):** This allows everyone — family, friends, complete strangers, ax murderers — to look at your photos.

    - • **My Network:** This allows only the people who are in your Windows Live Network to see the photos. (For more on the Windows Live Network, see Chapter 12.)

    - • **Just Me:** This allows only you to see the pictures.

    - • **Select People:** This allows you to define exactly who in your Windows Live Network can see the pictures.

Figure 10-9: Creating an album in Windows Live Photo Gallery.

A shared folder, like the album shown in Figure 10-10, is accessible to those who are authorized simply by sending them the link. Here's how:

1. **Take a photo with your phone.**

2. **Open the Pictures app on your phone and find the picture you just took in your All section.**

3. **Tap once on the photo to bring it to full size on the phone's screen.**

4. **Tap once on the full-size photo to bring up the menu options.**

5. **Tap on Share to Windows Live.**

   You're asked which album on Windows Live you want to place the photo in.

6. **Tap the album name.**

   Make sure the album has the access options you want, because as soon as you upload the photo to Windows Live, anyone who has access to that album can see it.

   A copy of the photo is automatically uploaded to your Windows Live account and placed in the album you specified.

Uploading photos to Windows Live Photo Gallery has a few advantages over just keeping your photos on your phone and, when you get around to it, downloading them to your PC through a USB cable:

- ✓ **You can store more pictures in your Windows Live Photo Gallery than you can on your phone.** Microsoft gives you 25 GB for storing photos, which is way more than you'd want to keep on your phone (if your phone even has 25 GB of space).

Figure 10-10: A sample album in Windows Live Photo Gallery.

✓ **The Windows Live Photo Gallery is backed up and protected.** If you lose your phone, all the photos that you've stored on it are lost, too. But if you've uploaded your photos to Windows Live Photo Gallery, they're safe.

✓ **Windows Live Photo Gallery allows you to share photos with as many friends as you want, without having to e-mail them the photos.** You don't want to be that annoying person who clogs everyone's inboxes with photos of your kids if they don't want to see the photos of your kids. By putting them on Windows Live Photo Gallery, your friends can see your photos when they want to (and not see them when they don't).

The albums that you create on your phone may or may not be the same as the albums that you create in Windows Live Photo Gallery. For example, you may have an album on your phone that's called "Honeymoon," with all the pictures from your honeymoon in one album. But you may not want everyone in your Windows Live Network to see every photo from your honeymoon. So, in Windows Live Photo Gallery, you could create one album called "Honeymoon: Private" and set it so that only you and your spouse can see those images, and have another album called "Honeymoon: Everyone" and allow everyone in your network to see those images. Just make sure you're crystal clear what the accessibility settings are for every album — unless you want to share every last bit of yourself with the world.

You can access the Windows Live Photo Gallery on your phone, but it may be more convenient to do it on your computer. Either way, the directions and the screens are the same.

11

Sending and Receiving
E-Mail on Your Phone

In This Chapter

▶ Setting up your e-mail accounts on your phone

▶ Reading e-mails on your phone

▶ Managing your e-mail folder

▶ Sending e-mails from your phone

*I*f you've had e-mail on your phone for a while, you know how convenient it is. If your new Windows Phone is the first cellphone you have with the capability to send and receive e-mail, prepare to be hooked.

I start this chapter by giving you the steps to follow to set up your e-mail, whether or not your e-mail is supported (more on that in a bit). Then I show you how to read and manage your e-mails. Finally, I tell you how to write and send e-mails.

Your phone primarily interacts with your inbox on your e-mail account. It isn't really set up to work like the full-featured e-mail application on your PC. Theoretically, you may never need to get on your PC to access your e-mail again, and you could store e-mails in folders on your phone. But the phone access to e-mail is best used in working with the e-mails that are in your inbox.

Setting Up Your E-Mail

To set up e-mail on your phone, go to the Start screen. Look for the Mail Setup tile; it has an envelope icon on it (see Figure 11-1).

Courtesy of Microsoft Corporation

Figure 11-1: The Mail Setup tile on the Start screen.

After you tap the Mail Setup tile, tap the Add an Account link. The screen shown in Figure 11-2 appears.

How you proceed from here depends on whether your e-mail account type is fully supported.

✓ **Fully supported:** The fully supported e-mail types are the ones you see in Figure 11-2:

  • Windows Live (including addresses ending in `msn.com`, `hotmail.com`, and `live.com`)

  • Outlook (accessed by Microsoft Outlook on your PC)

  • Yahoo!

Figure 11-2: The Add an Account screen.

✏ **Not fully supported:** Everything else. If your e-mail address ends in anything else, like gmail.com, aol.com, or comcast.net, it's not fully supported by the Windows Phone. Don't worry — you'll probably be able to access your e-mail following the steps in this section.

I walk you through both scenarios in this section.

Using a supported e-mail account

If you have a supported e-mail account, here's how to set up your account on your Windows Phone:

1. **From the Add an Account screen (refer to Figure 11-2), tap the icon that corresponds to your type of e-mail (for example, Windows Live or Yahoo!).**

A screen appears, asking you for your e-mail address and your password.

2. **Enter your e-mail address in the E-mail text box.**

3. **Enter your password in the Password text box.**

4. **Tap Submit.**

The synchronization process takes a little while, but within a minute or so, your e-mail account's inbox is present on your phone. That's it! You're done.

Using a non-fully-supported e-mail account

If you don't have a fully supported e-mail account, tap the Other Account link (refer to Figure 11-2). Similar to the preceding section, you're asked to enter your e-mail address and password. After you've done so, tap Submit.

Now, in most cases, you'll see a synchronization process begin. If you don't, you need to get some technical support from your e-mail service provider.

The Windows Phone e-mail app works with POP3-accessible accounts. This is far and away the most common kind of remote access for e-mail. This information helps tech support give you the information you need for synchronization with your e-mail account.

Setting up multiple accounts

The e-mail app on your phone works with multiple e-mail accounts. You can bring both your work and your personal e-mail together to work with your phone.

Before you set up your work e-mail on your phone, make sure you have permission to do so. If you do it without the green light from your company, and you end up violating your company's rules, you could be in hot water. Increasing your productivity won't be much help if you're standing out in the parking lot holding all the contents of your office in a cardboard box.

Reading E-Mail on Your Phone

The Windows Phone Inbox has three sections (see Figure 11-3):

- **All:** All the e-mails in your Inbox
- **Unread:** The e-mails that you haven't opened, either on your PC or on your phone

When you open an e-mail on your phone, it tells the e-mail client on your PC or on the Web (wherever your e-mail is stored) that you've opened the message.

✓ **Urgent:** The e-mails that were flagged as urgent by the people sending them

You navigate among the three sections by dragging the screen to the right or left.

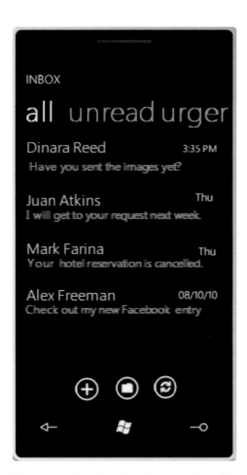

Figure 11-3: Your Inbox has three sections: All, Unread, and Urgent.

In Figure 11-3, you see several emails in the Inbox. Each e-mail shows the name of the sender, the e-mail's subject, and the first few words of the message itself. To read the entire email, you just tap that e-mail. This brings up the full e-mail message as shown in Figure 11-4.

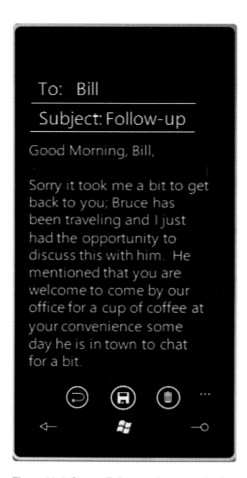

Figure 11-4: An email that you have received.

Toward the bottom of the screen are three icons:

- **Left arrow icon:** Reply to this sender.
- **Folder icon:** File this e-mail in a folder on the phone.
- **Recycling icon:** Delete this e-mail from your phone *and* your PC.

Just select the message, and tap the appropriate button.

Managing Your E-Mails

From the Inbox (refer to Figure 11-3), you can manage your e-mails. At the bottom of the screen are three icons. They have following functions:

- **Plus sign:** Tap to start a new e-mail message.
- **Folder:** When you tap this, you're taken to a screen that allows you to put an e-mail into
  - **Inbox:** Allows you to put e-mails that are stored in another folder back in your Inbox
  - **Drafts:** Stores partially completed e-mails that haven't been sent
  - **Show All Folders:** Opens all the folders that exist on your phone and creates a new folder if needed
- **Synchronize:** Tapping this icon causes your phone to recheck with your e-mail service to make sure that it has the latest update of your e-mails.

Instead of having to change the status of e-mails one at a time, you can change multiple e-mails at once:

1. **Tap the leftmost part of the screen.**

   All the e-mails shift to the right, and check boxes appear next to each e-mail.

2. **Tap the check boxes next to the messages that you want to make the same change to.**

3. **Tap the ellipsis.**

4. **Tap Delete, Mark as Unread, or Flag to make the change to all the checked e-mails.**

Writing and Sending an E-Mail

Tapping the plus sign (refer to Figure 11-3) brings up a blank e-mail template (shown in Figure 11-5).

At the top, in the To field, is where you type the address of the intended recipient. Below that, in the Subject field, is where you enter the subject of the e-mail. And below that is the body of the e-mail, with the default signature "Sent from my Windows Phone."

At the bottom of the screen are three icons and the ellipsis:

- **Trailing envelope:** Tapping this icon sends the e-mail to the intended recipient(s). It's basically a send button.
- **Paperclip:** Tap this to attach a file to your e-mail.

Figure 11-5: A new e-mail message.

✔ **X:** Tap this if you change your mind about writing an email. If you're partially done with the message, you're asked if you want to save it in your Drafts folder.

✔ **Ellipsis:** When you tap the ellipsis, you get two options:

 • **Show CC and BCC:** The default for an e-mail on your phone is to display just the intended recipient's e-mail address. If you want to carbon copy (CC) or blind carbon copy (BCC) other people, you can tap this option.

 • **Priority:** This allows you to set an e-mail message to high priority.

Keeping Connected with Your BFFs

In This Chapter

▶ Integrating your social networks on your phone

▶ Getting all your contacts in one location

▶ Keeping up to date with just a few taps

*O*ne of the focus areas that Microsoft spent a lot of time considering when creating this version of Windows Phone is to make it easier for you to communicate with your most important contacts — your family, friends, coworkers, customers, or whoever matters to you.

On most smartphones, including the Windows Phone, you may communicate with someone by

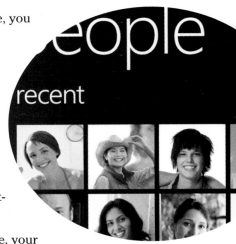

✔ Making a voice call to a home phone, a work phone, or a cellphone

✔ Sending a text message to another cellphone

✔ Sending an instant message (IM) to a computer

✔ E-mailing a personal address or work address

✔ E-mailing through a social networking site

✔ Monitoring your friends' updates on a social networking site

On all other smartphones except the Windows Phone, your communications are organized by technology, and not necessarily according to how you'd want to use them. So, if you want to talk to someone, you bring up the Phone application. If you then want to text someone, you close the Phone app and open the Text app. If you want to e-mail someone, you close the Text app and bring up your E-mail app.

What your Windows Phone offers is a way to do all these things from one place, the People hub (shown in Figure 12-1). The menus on the People hub include the following:

- ✔ **Recent:** The eight most recent people you've communicated with

- ✔ **All:** Your entire contact database, including a picture of each person (see Figure 12-2)

- ✔ **What's New:** The most recent e-mails, texts, or social networking comments from people within your contact database, listed in reverse chronological order.

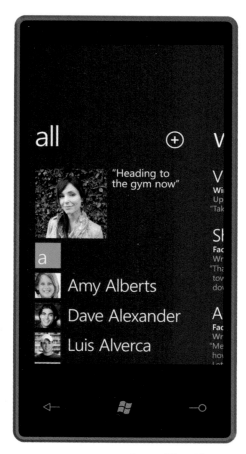

Courtesy of Microsoft Corporation

Figure 12-1: The People hub.

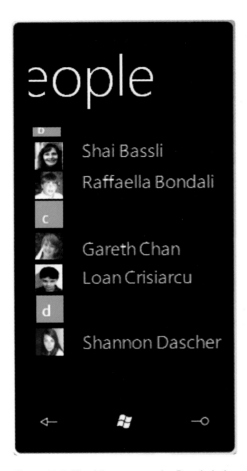

Figure 12-2: The All screen on the People hub.

All the communications options available are at one site that's constantly monitoring for you any communications coming from that person so that you communicate back to that person.

The People hub is kind of like a contact database on steroids. To put it to work for you, you just need to set up a few things on your phone and on Windows Live. In this chapter, I walk you through the steps to take.

Setting Up Your Social Networks

Just as you can add an e-mail account to your phone, you can also add social networks. In Chapter 11, I walk you through setting up an e-mail account.

You may have noticed that one of the account type options is Facebook. Windows Phone makes it super-easy to add Facebook. In this section, I show you how. I also walk you through adding your other social networking sites.

Facebook

Here's how to add Facebook to your Windows Phone:

1. **Press the Start button to get to the Start screen on your phone.**

2. **Tap the Mail Setup tile (refer to Figure 11-1).**

3. **Tap the Add an Account link.**

   The screen shown in Figure 11-2 appears.

4. **Tap the Facebook icon.**

   A screen appears asking you for your Facebook ID (which is the e-mail address associated with your Facebook account) and you Facebook password.

5. **Enter your Facebook ID in the appropriate text box.**

6. **Enter your password in the Password text box.**

7. **Tap Submit.**

The synchronization process begins and, within about a minute, messages, pictures, and comments from your Facebook account appear on your phone. Without your having to do anything more, the photos that you've loaded on to Facebook are now in the Pictures hub!

Other social networking sites

As with non-supported email accounts, tap Other Account. You're asked to enter your e-mail address and password. In this case, use your log-in ID and password. When you are done, tap Submit.

In most cases, a synchronization process begins. If not, you need to get some help from technical support from your social-networking service provider.

Over time, Microsoft in partnership with social networking sites will add more sites, like Twitter, MySpace, and LinkedIn. The sooner the better.

Setting Up Your Contact Database

You're probably familiar with using contact databases. Many cellphones automatically create one. You probably have one on your work computer, comprised of work e-mail addresses and telephone numbers. And if you have a personal e-mail account, you probably have a contact database of e-mail accounts of friends and family members. If you're kickin' it old school, you may even keep a paper address book with names, addresses, and telephone numbers.

The problem with having all these contact databases is that it's rarely ever as neat and tidy as I've just outlined. A friend may e-mail you at work, so you have her in both your contact databases. Then her e-mail address may change, and you may remember to update that information in your personal address book but not in your work one. Before long, you've got duplicated contacts and out-of-date contacts, and it's hard to tell which is correct.

Windows Live lets you integrate all your electronic contact databases. This way, you can have it automatically update the contact database on your phone.

You don't have to use Windows Live for this if you don't want to. You can build the contact database on your Windows Phone the same way that you've built up your contacts on phones before: a combination of manually entering the data onto your phone and adding numbers of people as they call you. This approach works, too — it just isn't as slick.

I cover the manual approach first, because it's easy to explain. Then I cover the process for automatically keeping your contact files current.

Microsoft calls a contact database "People" and each record a "Profile."

Adding pictures to your Profiles

You can easily add pictures to the contacts on your phone. Choose one of the following options:

✔ From the Profile of an individual on your phone, tap the photo icon and insert an image from the photos on your phone.

✔ From the Profile of an individual on your PC, click the photo icon and insert an image from the photos on your PC.

✔ From a picture stored on your phone, tap on the ellipsis to get sorting options. Tap the Assign to a Contact option, which brings up all your contacts. Tap the contact you want this picture to be assigned to.

Pretty simple.

Adding contacts to your phone manually

This process takes an existing contact database and enters it to your Windows Phone, one profile at a time.

1. **Tap the People tile.**

   The screen shown in Figure 12-3 appears.

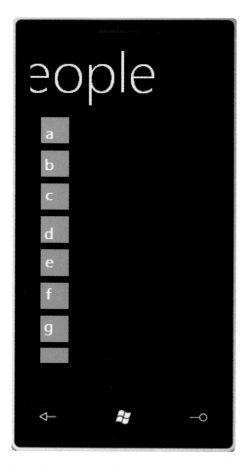

Figure 12-3: An empty People hub.

2. **Tap the plus sign.**

   A screen with text boxes appears.

3. **Fill in the information that you want to include.**

4. **Tap the Save icon.**

The profile is now on your phone. Repeat the process for as many profiles as you want to create.

Adding contacts as you communicate

When you receive a call, text, or e-mail from someone who isn't in your People, you're given the option to create a Profile for that person. The same is true when you initiate contact with someone who isn't in your People. Figure 12-4 shows the phone dialing a number. After you dial the number, you have the option to save the phone number. When you tap Save, the profile template is populated with that number — you just need to add the name and any other contact information associated with that number.

Figure 12-4: The phone dialer with the Save option at the bottom.

Similarly, when you're working with e-mails (refer to Chapter 11), if your phone doesn't recognize an e-mail address, a Save icon appears, allowing you to create a profile for that person.

Importing data from your SIM card

If your phone uses a SIM card (shown in Figure 12-5), which is the case if your cellular carrier is AT&T, T-Mobile, or US Cellular, you can import your contacts from your old phone.

Figure 12-5: A standard SIM card.

If you're on Verizon or Sprint Nextel, you don't have a SIM card.

To import the contact data from the SIM card into your People list on your phone, follow these steps:

1. **Tap the People tile.**

2. **Tap the Import SIM Contacts link.**

   All the information you had on your old phone is moved onto your new phone.

Check the profiles to make sure that your phone populated the correct fields. The conversion process is very good, but it's not perfect.

Building contacts with Windows Live

You can set up a connection between the People application on your phone and the People application on Windows Live. When this is fully implemented, the following things automatically take place:

✔ When you update the information in the profile of one of your friends on your phone, it automatically updates the profile in Windows Live and on your PC.

✔ When you update contact information on your PC, your phone updates automatically.

✔ If you invite a friend to connect with you through Windows Live, when he updates his information, it automatically updates your Windows Live and your phone.

✔ Windows Live can import your contact databases that you've stored in your computer in Microsoft Office formats.

✔ Windows Live can import your friends from any of the following social networking sites:

- Facebook

- MySpace

- AOL

- Hyves

- Hi5

✔ Windows Live can automatically sort out the duplicate information from the different sources and give you a single profile for each person.

In the following sections, I walk you through setting up Windows Live to populate your phone and your Windows Live People application.

Making the connection between your phone and Windows Live People

You set up the connection from the phone by opening the People app and tapping Set up Account.

You'll be asked to verify that you want to synchronize the profiles, and — poof! — you're connected. Your phone populates your Windows Live People information with its information. If you have information in your Windows Live contact list, it updates your phone.

From the Windows Live home screen, click Contacts. This takes you to the screen shown in Figure 12-6.

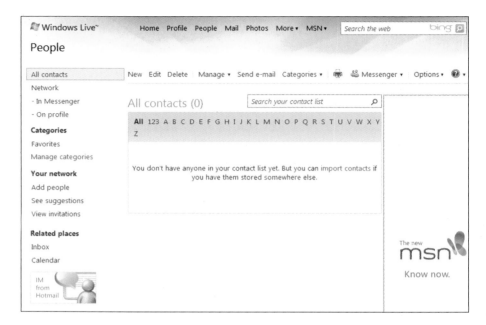

Figure 12-6: The People screen in Windows Live.

You can do all this from your phone, but it's easier to do from your PC.

Adding people from your PC

To add people from your PC to your phone, from the Windows Live People screen (refer to Figure 12-6), click the Add People link. The screen shown in Figure 12-7 appears.

Figure 12-7: The Add People option within the Windows Live People screen.

There are two options for adding people to your contacts: Social Networks and Exported Files. So, as you may have guessed, you can add contacts either from your social networks on your PC or from the files on your PC.

Inviting people from your social networks

To add contacts from your social networks, the first step is to select which social network you want to import from. For demonstration purposes, I'll walk you through importing from Facebook:

1. **When you click Facebook, you see the screen shown in Figure 12-8, where you verify that you're okay with this.**

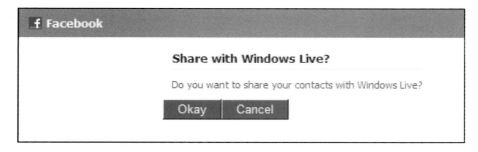

Figure 12-8: Facebook verification that you're okay with sharing.

You're asked whether you want to add the people who are already on Windows Live (see Figure 12-9).

2. **Select the ones you want to add, and click Next.**

Figure 12-9: A screen that checks whether you're okay adding people on Windows Live.

Windows Live asks whether you want to invite the people who aren't on Windows Live if they want to join (see Figure 12-10).

3. **Again, select the people you want to invite, and click Next.**

Figure 12-10: A screen that checks whether you want to add people who are *not* on Windows Live.

4. **In the last step, you actually invite all these people to be in your Windows Live Network (as shown in Figure 12-11).**

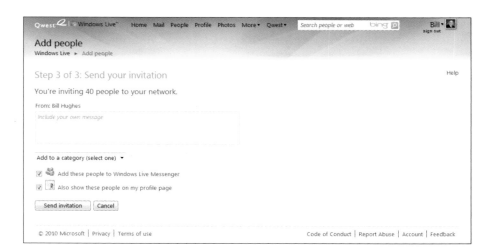

Figure 12-11: Sending an invitation to join your network.

The invitation looks like Figure 12-12.

When they accept, all the information you have for these people will be moved into Profiles.

This sounds too good to be true

Integrating with Windows Live addresses all the issues that come from carrying duplicate contact databases. Actually, it's almost as good as it sounds. But you may face a few issues during the process:

✔ If you have a friend who has multiple first names, like Bill and Billy, you need to pick one or the other.

✔ If you have multiple people that share common information, like the Jones family e-mail account, but you also have individual contact information for each member of the Jones family, the profile structure doesn't know how to handle it and will take a guess.

Otherwise, the system works as advertised, and the information flows into your PC or phone with no intervention on your part!

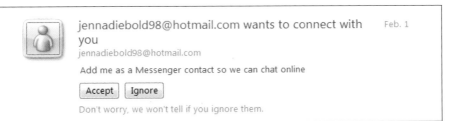

Figure 12-12: An invitation to join your network.

Converting your existing e-mail contacts

To get contacts from your PC to your phone, from the screen in Figure 12-7, click Import Contacts. You go through the same steps you do for importing from social networks (see the preceding section).

Navigating Your People Hub

After people accept your invitation, they're in your network. They can see what's going on with you and you can see what's new with them. And all this information is brought together on your People hub. Refer to Figure 12-1 for a look at the panorama for the People hub.

The Recent screen shows the eight most recent people with whom you've communicated. To contact one of those people again, you tap her image and her Profile comes up, as shown in Figure 12-13. In addition to the person's photo, you see all her contact information. To call her, you tap Call Mobile. To text her, you tap Text Mobile.

Figure 12-13: A typical Profile.

The All screen is your entire contact database. You flick down or up to get to the contact you want. Tapping on that person's image brings up her most current Profile. Tap how you want to communicate with her or just see what's new in the "What's New" section of her profile (shown in Figure 12-14).

Figure 12-14: What's New for an individual.

You can add any of your contacts on your home page. On each Profile, you see a pin icon (refer to Figure 12-14). When you tap the pin icon, that person becomes a tile on your home page — and she's never more than a few quick taps away.

Part V
Music and Videos in the Palm of Your Hand

The 5th Wave   By Rich Tennant

"You ever notice how much more streaming media there is than there used to be?"

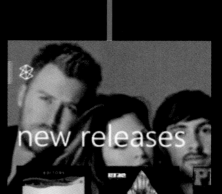

In this part . . .

You may not have known this, but your Windows Phone uses the Zune technology, one of the most advanced mobile entertainment systems currently available. For the cost of a subscription, you have a powerful portable entertainment system in the palm of your hand. In this part, you find out how to add music and videos to your phone, and how to play them once they're there.

The "Phonified" Zune HD

In This Chapter

▶ Appreciating the Zune multimedia experience

▶ Navigating through music and video on your phone

M ost smartphones have built-in digital music players, but your Windows Phone has a Zune HD built in to it, which is far and away more exciting! Zune HD has many more features than a run-of-the-mill MP3 player, and in this chapter, I fill you in. Although the functionality of the Windows Phone is not identical to the Zune HD, there are numerous similarities (and I point out the differences in this chapter).

Recognizing What Zune HD Can Do

Microsoft's Zune HD is much more capable than a run-of-the-mill MP3 player. Microsoft has put a considerable amount of thought and work into making the Zune more than a jukebox for digital music files. Here's what sets the Zune experience apart from a typical MP3 player that plays music and videos:

- ✔ **Sharing communities:** Microsoft promotes Zune with its concept called the "Social." This means two things:

  - **Sharing files with friends:** You can share music files with friends for a limited number of plays and/or plays direct from one Zune player to another Zune player without having to connect through a PC.

  - **Communities of fans with similar tastes:** You can link up with people who like similar music to keep you aware of new songs or groups.

- ✔ **Sharing suggestions:** An automated system makes suggestions for you based on your history of listening to music tracks.

- ✔ **Playlists:** A *playlist* is a group of similar songs that follow a related theme. You can create your own playlist with any songs you want or you can acquire premade playlists. More on that later.

- ✔ **HD radio:** If you have not listened to the sound of HD radio, you're missing a wonderful experience. It is all right there on your Windows Phone. *Note:* Not all Windows Phones come with HD radios. The HD radio is optional and left up to the manufacturer.

- ✔ **Overdesigned components:** In many cases, having a device that uses components that are better than necessary just adds cost. In this case, however, you can expect that Microsoft will be adding additional capabilities to the phone that will bring it up to the capabilities of the Zune HD.

TECHNICAL STUFF

What your phone can't do (yet)

The Zune HD, Microsoft's answer to Apple's iPod, can do the following things that your Windows Phone can't do (yet):

- ✔ **Load digital music from your CD collection:** If you already have a license for a song/album for your personal use, as you do with CDs you've purchased, you can load that song/album to your Zune HD. But you won't be able to do this with your Windows Phone, unless your phone's manufacturer enables this (a cable connection between your PC and your phone is optional).

- ✔ **Dock with a full stereo with a dock:** You can connect a Zune HD to your full stereo, which is easier than pulling out a CD and putting it in your CD player. Also, your tuner may not support HD radio, but Zune HD has that. The only way to dock your Windows Phone with a full stereo is to use the headphone jack. It works, but it is not as "clean" as having an A/V dock.

- ✔ **Play HD movies on a full-screen TV:** You can load several full HD movies on your Zune HD and drive your HD TV. Unfortunately, you can't do that with your Windows Phone.

Feel like I'm torturing you with this information on what your Windows Phone can't do? Here's why you may want to know this information:

- ✔ **The software and hardware platforms for the Zune HD and the Windows Phone are closely related.** Although Microsoft bristled at the Windows Phone being called a Zune phone, this term really is more accurate than not.

- ✔ **A Zune Marketplace subscription applies to both your Zune and your phone.** The music you buy from the Zune Marketplace is for up to three Zune players and/or Windows Phones. This flexibility encourages you to get a Zune or a second Windows Phone for a close friend or family member to share your one Zune Marketplace subscription.

The hardware components are there in the Windows Phone, so I wouldn't be surprised if the Windows Phone eventually has these features. In the meantime, you get the Zune experience on better-quality sound components than you would with a standard MP3 player.

Navigating Music and Video on Your Windows Phone

The Zune experience starts at the start screen with the Music + Video tile (shown in Figure 13-1).

Courtesy of Microsoft Corporation

Figure 13-1: The Music + Video tile on the start screen.

Tap the Music + Video tile, and you're taken to the Music + Video panorama (shown in Figure 13-2). As you can see in Figure 13-2, there are four main parts in the panorama:

 ✔ The Zune start screen (on the far left)

 ✔ History

 ✔ New

 ✔ Apps

Courtesy of Microsoft Corporation

Figure 13-2: The Music + Video panorama.

In this section, I cover each of these parts in greater detail.

The Zune start screen

The first screen you see in the Music + Video panorama is the Zune start screen (shown in Figure 13-3). This is the Zune start screen. Each one of the words is a link to launch a new Zune experience. Here you have the following choices:

 ✔ **Music:** Tap this to play music stored on your phone.

 ✔ **Videos:** Tap this to play a video stored on your phone.

 ✔ **Podcasts:** Tap this to play a podcast stored on your phone.

   Podcasts are stored in the same format as music files, but keeping podcasts in a separate filing system from your music is convenient.

 ✔ **Radio:** Tap this to access the FM and HD radio.

 ✔ **Marketplace:** Tap this to go to the Marketplace, where you can buy and download music, albums, videos, and podcasts. (For more on the Zune Marketplace, turn to Chapter 14.)

In Chapter 8, I covered the Windows Phone Marketplace, where you can go to buy apps for your phone. In reality, it's all connected, but when you come in to the Marketplace from the Music + Video panorama, it assumes that you're looking for music and videos.

Courtesy of Microsoft Corporation

Figure 13-3: The Zune start screen is where it all starts.

Tapping the Music, Videos, or Podcasts link takes you to the music library on your phone. (Chapter 15 explains how to navigate your multimedia libraries as well as use the radio.)

Delving into your past with the History screen

The first screen to the right of the Zune start screen is the History screen (see Figure 13-4), which lists all the songs you've played most recently on your phone. The History screen is updated constantly, as your playing habits change. Flick to the right to see more of your history.

Courtesy of Microsoft Corporation

Figure 13-4: The History screen tells you where you've been.

Finding music you've recently downloaded on the New screen

To the right of the History screen is the list of new songs you've downloaded to your phone (see Figure 13-5). When you start adding songs from the Zune Marketplace, this section of the panorama displays those songs in the order in which you've added them.

Courtesy of Microsoft Corporation

Figure 13-5: The New screen shows you what you've downloaded recently.

Working the Zune Marketplace

In This Chapter
▶ Knowing your licensing options
▶ Finding your next favorite song or video

*T*he ultimate goal of the Zune Marketplace is to introduce you to as much new music and videos as possible, so that you can get the most enjoyment out of your listening and viewing experience. The Zune Marketplace makes it convenient for you to put music and videos on your phone. In this chapter, I explain the differences between the different types of licensing (it sounds more complicated than it is), tell you how set your payment options, and guide you to finding the music and videos you want.

Listening Up on Licensing

When you buy music or videos in the Zune Marketplace, you're essentially buying a "license" for that music or those videos. Just putting music or videos on your phone isn't enough — you have to have the authorization to play them. In this section, I cover your options for music and videos.

Music and podcasts

There are two licensing options available with the Windows Phone for music files and podcasts:

✓ **Points:** With Points, you pay for each file individually. Instead of having lots of small transactions each time you buy a multimedia file, the Marketplace uses a point system (see Figure 14-1). You can buy 400 points for $5, and you don't get any discounts if you buy more points at once. Buying a typical song will deduct 79 points from your account, which works out to be 99¢. Buying a typical album will deduct 1,000 points, which is the equivalent of $12.50.

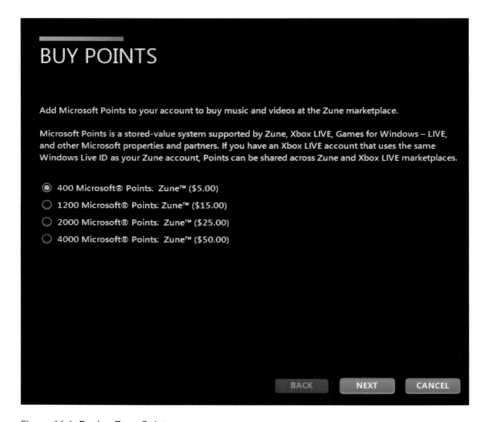

Figure 14-1: Buying Zune Points.

The Points don't apply just to multimedia files. You also use them for video and Xbox LIVE purchases. (For more on Xbox LIVE, turn to Chapter 16.)

✔ **Zune Pass:** The other option for buying music is the Zune Pass. For $14.99 per month, you can download as much music as you want from the Zune library to your phone.

The Zune Pass gives you complete access to all the music files on Zune, but it doesn't give you unlimited access to other services, such as videos or Xbox LIVE games.

Doing the math on the Zune Pass

When you're first getting started, you may want to play it safe and start with Points. That way, if you end up not using the service much on your phone, you're only out the $5 you spent on the first 400 points. The thing is, Microsoft is aware of that, so they've done what some restaurants do, and priced the all-you-can-eat buffet at just about what you would pay for a meal and beverages.

If you take advantage of downloading the ten free songs with your Zune Pass, instead of $14.99 for the month, you're paying only about $5 more for the ability to listen to the entire Zune library: $14.99 − (10 × $0.99 per song) = $5.09. This perspective makes is hard to pass up the Zune Pass.

The "catch" is that if you don't renew the Zune Pass, the license to the music on your phone, except for the ten songs per month that you explicitly purchased, will expire. It'll still be there, but your phone won't allow you to play it. If you buy another Zune Pass, you'll be able to play it again, but without the need to download the file.

In addition, Microsoft has been running a promotion where you get two weeks of Zune Pass for free. If this promotion is available, it also can give you a taste of what's available. (Note that the promotion does not offer you the option of free songs, and there's no guarantee the promotion will be running when you read this.)

In addition to full access to the music library, the Zune Pass offers:

- **Special services:** Channels, Mixview, and Smart DJ are optimized to take advantage of unlimited access to music capabilities. Channels is a continuously updated playlist in a particular music genre; the songs on the playlist are updated as new songs become available, just to keep the channel fresh. Mixview shows other tracks and artists that are similar to the music that's currently playing; you can tap on a different song and be taken to that track. Smart DJ is like Mixview, but it creates and launches a playlist based on an album, artist, or song stored on your phone rather than what's playing at the moment.

These services are a very convenient way to learn about new music. If you have even a small interest in expanding your music repertoire, these services are an easy way to do it.

- **Multiple devices on the same Zune Pass:** Up to three computers and three devices can use the same Zune Pass.

- **Ten free songs per month:** If you intend to keep paying $14.99 forever, this won't mean much to you. But if you plan to take breaks from time to time, this option allows you to stock up on songs that you like. The ten free downloads must be stored to your phone every month — you can't wait, say, three months and then download 30 songs.

Which option is most economical depends on your listening/viewing habits. If you don't plan to buy much, or you know specifically what you want, you may save some money by paying for all your files individually. If you're not really sure what you want, or you like a huge variety of things, paying for monthly access may make sense for you.

Videos

There are two licensing options available for videos on the Windows Phone:

- ✔ **Rental:** You can view the video for 24 hours from the start of the first play, as long as this is within 14 days of your first downloading it. When you rent, you have two resolution options, depending on which device you intend to play the video on:

  - **SD Resolution:** *SD* stands for standard definition. This is a lower-cost rental and uses a smaller file. SD is fine if you're only going to run the video on your phone or your Zune (if you have one). An SD-resolution rental costs 320 Zune Points, or the equivalent of $4.

  - **HD Resolution:** *HD* stands for high definition. If you have a Zune HD with an audio/video dock, this allows you to connect it to your HD-TV and get the kind of picture you're after. An HD-resolution rental costs 480 Zune Points, or the equivalent of $6.

- ✔ **Purchase:** You have a license to view the file as frequently as you want, for as long as you want. A purchase costs 1,200 Zune Points, or the equivalent of $15.

It makes sense to buy the video if you'll watch it several times or if you may not be able to finish watching it within the rental time limit.

Handing Over Your Hard-Earned Money

To get Points or a Zune Pass, you need to hand over your credit card information.

Here's how:

1. **From the start screen on the Zune panorama (refer to Figure 14-2), tap the Marketplace link.**

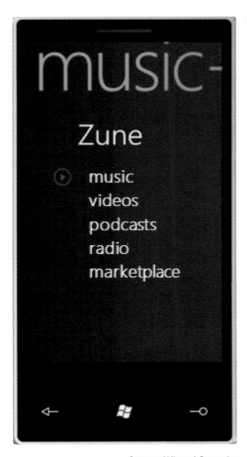

Figure 14-2: The Zune start screen.

You get a screen similar to the one shown in Figure 14-3.

Figure 14-3: The Zune Marketplace screen.

2. Tap the ellipsis at the bottom of the screen.

3. Tap Account.

You're asked to create a Zune account with information shown in Figure 14-4. Then you're asked to agree to the terms of service. The lawyers say that you should read this before you sign it.

Figure 14-4: The Zune Account Info screen.

4. **The next screen asks you some questions about your interest in getting updates and participating in the social aspects of the Zune Service. Answer these any way that you prefer.**

5. **Enter your Zune tag (see Figure 14-5), and tap Next.**

   The Zune tag is how you communicate to others in the Zune social space. It's more expedient and private than typing your entire e-mail address. Choose a name that's easy for you to remember.

Figure 14-5: Creating your Zune tag.

6. **Enter your contact information.**

7. **Enter your credit card number.**

8. **Tap Finish.**

You now have a choice to buy a Zune Pass or Points.

Getting Music and Videos

When you know what you want — what you really, really want — here's how you download it:

1. **Press the hardware Search button.**

   A search box pops up.

2. **Tap in the name of the artist or song.**

   You see a series of options (shown in Figure 14-6). In this case, I tapped in Spice Girls, and I can choose among:

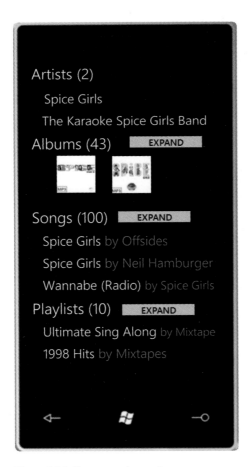

Figure 14-6: Zune search results.

- Artists with Spice Girls in the name
- Songs by the Spice Girls
- Albums by the Spice Girls
- A bio of the Spice Girls
- A playlist that includes the Spice Girls
- Videos of the Spice Girls
- Zune tabs of other members who are fans of the Spice Girls

3. **Because you know what you want, what you really, really want — the song "Wannabe" — you tap Songs.**

   This brings up the list of songs shown in Figure 14-7.

Figure 14-7: The Spice Girls songs list.

4. **Flick down to find the song you want.**

   "Wannabe" is high on the list, so you don't have to flick down to it.

5. **Tap the song when you find it.**

   The price is set at 79 points. If you have a Zune Pass, nothing is deducted. If you use Zune Points, 79 points are deducted from your balance.

   The download begins. Within a few seconds, the song is in your library.

6. **To play the song, tap the song's icon.**

You may notice that the screens are very graphically intensive and offer you lots of options to learn more, download a complete album, and find out about similar songs.

Buying an entire album is a little cheaper than buying individual songs. If you buy a song, and then you buy the entire album, you still need to pay the full price for the album. You don't get credit for the song you already purchased.

Here are your options for learning about new songs:

- ✓ The Channels, Mixview, and Smart DJ applications (mentioned earlier in this chapter)
- ✓ The album history of the artist

✔ Featured artists in the Marketplace (see Figure 14-8)

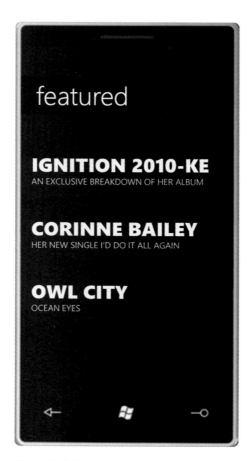

Figure 14-8: Zune Marketplace featured artists.

✒ Newly released songs (see Figure 14-9)

Figure 14-9: Zune Marketplace newly released songs.

 ✒ Newly released albums (see Figure 14-10)

Figure 14-10: Zune Marketplace newly released albums.

✔ Top-selling albums (see Figure 14-11)

Figure 14-11: Zune Marketplace top-selling albums.

✔ Music genres (see Figure 14-12)

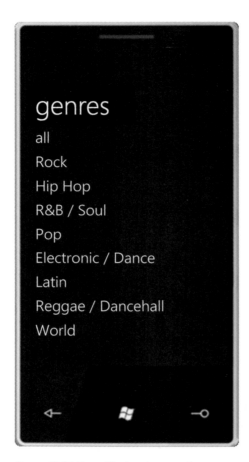

Figure 14-12: Zune Marketplace music genres.

✔ Playlists

Finding music that resonates with you is more of an art than a science. Zune Marketplace works all the angles to help you find new songs and albums that you'll like.

Playing Music and Videos

*C*hapter 14 walks you through downloading multimedia files. Now all you need to know is how to play them. In this chapter, I walk you through playing music, videos, podcasts, and radio. In each case, the instructions start at the Zune start screen (shown in Figure 15-1).

Playing Zune Tunes

When you want to play music on your Windows phone, you have three options: You can play a single song, a collection of songs, or a playlist. In the following sections, I walk you through each option.

Playing a single song

Let's go through what it would take to play a single song. For the sake of example, let's assume you want to play the single song "Single" by New Kids on the Block, from their album *The Block*. Follow these steps:

1. From the Zune start screen, tap Music.

You're taken to a panorama of your music, categorized in one of the following ways:

- By song title (see Figure 15-2)
- By album
- By genre
- By artist
- By playlist

2. **To bring up the song "Single," flick the screen down until you find the song title, and then tap it.**

   The screen shown in Figure 15-3 appears, giving you several options:

Courtesy of Microsoft Corporation

Figure 15-1: You play multimedia from the Zune start screen.

Figure 15-2: Zune songs listing.

- **Play:** Plays the song
- **Add to Now Playing:** Adds this song to the Now Playing playlist
- **Send:** Allows you to share this song with a friend

3. **Tap Play.**

   The album cover associated with the song pops up, and the song starts playing (see Figure 15-4). This screen gives you several pieces of information:

- **Timers:** How many minutes and seconds the song has been playing and how many minutes and seconds are left

- **Song information:** The song's title, the album, and the artist

- **Control keys:** The soft buttons on the bottom of the screen. They include from left to right: Shuffle (this should be grayed out and nonfunctional, because you've selected only one song), Repeat (gives you the option of repeating the song indefinitely), Restart (brings the song back to the start), Pause or Play (pauses or plays the song), and Fast Forward (takes you to the end of the song).

If you let the song reach the end, it stops there, unless you've tapped Repeat.

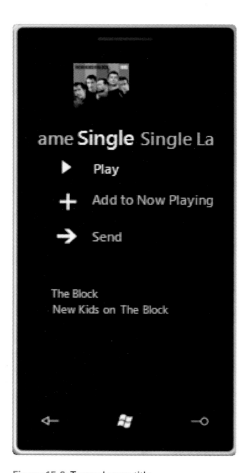

Figure 15-3: Tapped song title.

Figure 15-4: The screen when the song "Single" is playing.

Playing an album, artist, or genre

You may want to play just one song, but if you want music to keep on coming without your having to select one song at a time, you can play an entire album, all the songs from a particular artist, or all the songs from a particular genre of music.

1. **From the Zune start screen (refer to Figure 15-1), tap Music.**

   You're taken to a panorama of your music, categorized in one of the following sort options:

   - By song title
   - By album

- By genre
- By artist
- By playlist

2. **Depending on which sort option you want, pan to the left or right.**

   As you pan, you'll find that the active sort option (Album, Artist, Genre, Song, or Playlist) on the leftmost part of the screen is brighter white than the other sort options. That is the sort option that's active at the moment. The Albums, Artists, Genres, or whatever is appropriate for that sort option appears on the screen in alphabetic order.

3. **Flick down to the desired option (Album, Artist, Genre), and tap the link that you want to play. (You are almost there!)**

   Several options appear:

   - **Play All:** Plays all the songs in the category you've chosen
   - **Add to Now Playing:** Adds this selection, to the Now Playing playlist
   - **Send:** Allows you to share this selection with a friend

4. **Tap Play All.**

   The album cover associated with the first song on the list pops up, and the first song starts playing.

   All the songs on the list play through until the end of the last song is reached.

If you want the songs to keep on coming, you can tap the Shuffle key. This plays songs from the album, artist, genre, or playlist randomly, without stopping. The Shuffle key is a soft key on the screen.

Playing a playlist

A *playlist* is a series of songs. You can buy pre-packaged playlists on the Zune Marketplace or make your own playlists. Think of playlists as albums that you or someone other than the recording artist has created.

1. **From the Zune start screen, tap Music.**

2. **Touch Songs, and pan to the left or right to get to where is says Playlists; then drag Playlists to the left part of the screen.**

   The current playlists are displayed in alphabetic order.

3. **Pan or flick down to the desired playlist and tap it.**

   The following options appear:

   - **Play All:** Plays all the songs on the playlist
   - **Add to Now Playing:** Adds to the Now Playing playlist (*Note:* This option is not present for the Now Playing playlist.)
   - **Send:** Allows you to share this song with a friend

   In addition, you see the list of songs in the playlist.

4. **Tap Play All.**

   The album cover associated with the first song on the playlist pops up, and the first song starts playing. The album cover changes as each new song plays.

Playing Zune Videos

There are several similarities between playing music and playing videos. The main difference is that there are fewer categories for videos than music. This makes sense — you typically store fewer videos than you do songs. The categories for videos are

- **All:** All the videos on your phone
- **Music:** The music videos on your phone
- **Movies:** All the videos that aren't music videos

The steps to launch a movie are as follows:

1. **From the Zune start screen, tap Video.**

   The first sorting category is All. If you want to work with a shorter list, pan to the Music or Movie category.

2. **Pan or flick to get to the video that you want. When you find it, tap it.**

   The screen that appears gives you two choices:

   - **Resume:** Plays the video from where you last stopped watching. If you haven't yet started the video, it start at the beginning.
   - **Play from the Beginning:** Starts the video from the beginning.

3. **Tap either Resume or Play from the Beginning.**

   The video starts playing in landscape mode.

If you need to get to the play controls, such as Pause, Stop, or Fast Forward, tap the bottom of the screen, and they appear.

Playing Zune Podcasts

Playing a podcast is most like playing a single song:

1. **From the Zune start screen, tap Podcast.**

   A list of your podcasts appears.

2. **Pan or flick down to get the podcast title that you want, and tap that link.**

   This gives you two options:

   - **Play:** Plays the podcast
   - **Send:** Allows you to share the podcast with a friend

3. **Tap Play.**

   The Zune logo appears where the album cover for a song would appear. The podcast starts playing.

   This screen displays several pieces of information:

   - **Timers:** How many minutes and seconds the podcast has been playing and how many minutes and seconds are left

   - **Podcast author information**

   - **Control keys:** These are the soft buttons on the bottom of the screen. They include from left to right: Restart (brings the podcast back to the start), Pause/Play (pauses or plays the podcast), and Fast Forward (takes you to the end of the podcast).

   When the podcast reaches the end, it stops.

Playing Zune Radio

The FM radio in the Zune is a nice touch, but the HD radio is a wonderful addition. Your local FM stations broadcast to your radio in the same way they always have to your stereo receiver or car radio — it sounds good, and a lot better than AM radio, but it still has a fair amount of noise. But with an HD radio, that same radio station comes through without any imperfections.

Not all Windows Phones come with HD radios. The HD radio is optional and left up to the manufacturer.

The magic of HD

Through some technological magic, your local radio station is using the same frequency it always has to send the plain old FM radio broadcast plus up to three digital stations. The three radio stations on a given frequency are HD1, HD2, and HD3.

Typically, HD1 is just the digitized version of the broadcast FM radio. For example, let say that the radio station in your area on frequency 94.7 has call letters WINP and plays classic rock. If you have a regular, old FM radio, you'll receive it just as you always have. If you have an HD radio (which you do in your Windows Phone), 94.7 HD1 will be that same station, but broadcast digitally. It'll sound better the moment that

the HD radio receiver gets enough data to begin playing. If you're in good HD coverage area, this is typically just a few seconds.)

What happens is that you tune to 94.7 on the radio dial, and it sounds like normal FM. A few seconds later, you notice that sound will improve and the little HD1 icon appears (see the figure).

The music that plays on 94.7 HD2 and 94.7 HD3 are typically of a similar genre to the broadcast on 94.7, but this is entirely up to the station. A classic rock station could offer hip-hop on its HD2 and comedy on HD3.

To get to the FM and HD radios, from the Zune start screen, tap Radio. A radio tuner screen appears. If it happens not to be on an active radio station, it automatically finds one. If that particular FM station happens to have an HD offering, it automatically goes to HD1.

The music or talk station plays until you tap the arrow button or press the home button. Tapping the arrow button returns you to the Zune start screen.

Just because this is the first radio station that you found doesn't mean that you want to listen to it. Changing the radio station involves the following steps:

1. **Tap the station number.**

   This brings up double arrowheads (shown in Figure 15-5), which are tuning icons.

Figure 15-5: Zune HD station with tuning icons.

2. **To get a station with a higher number, tap the arrows pointing to the right. To get a station with a lower number, tap the arrows pointing to the left.**

   It doesn't matter if the station is in FM or HD mode.

To get to the other HD stations, tap the HD number you want. For example, if you're listening to HD1 and you want HD2, just tap on HD2.

It may take a second or two for the new HD station to get enough data to produce music. HD1 plays regular FM until it has enough data. HD2 and HD3 do not have that convenience for you, so you just need to be patient.

Part VI

Gaming on Your Phone with Xbox LIVE

In this part . . .

Microsoft's Xbox is a leading gaming console, loved globally by gamers. More recently, this experience has been supplemented with Xbox LIVE, an Internet-based service that expands the options for gamers. Xbox LIVE allows you to download new games for your console, engage in multi-player games, and compete with others from around the world.

With a Windows Phone, you can now take this experience with you when you're away from your console. You can play Xbox wherever you go, as long as your Windows phone goes with you.

In this part, I help you get started with Xbox LIVE and introduce you to some games for your Windows Phone.

16

Let the Games Begin!

Games are the most popular kind of download for smartphones of all kinds. In spite of the focus on business productivity, socializing, and making your life simpler, games outpace all other application downloads. You may be surprised to learn that the electronic gaming industry has larger revenues than the movie industry — and it has for several years!

The fact of the matter is that your Windows Phone is meant to leverage Microsoft's highly popular Xbox and Xbox LIVE services. Put another way, anyone who is more than just a casual Xbox fan should trade in his old phone and pick up a new Windows Phone. Because you already have one, let's concentrate on having fun!

Figuring Out What to Play: Game Types

The games category is a huge one, and it includes everything from simple puzzles to simulated violence. All games involve various combinations of intellect, skill (either competitive or motor), and role playing. In Xbox LIVE, games are divided into the following genres:

- **Card and board games:** These are electronic versions of familiar — and some not so familiar — board and card games. For example, an application that plays Texas Hold 'em would be in this category.

- **Educational:** Educational games are meant to be enjoyable *and* offer the users enhanced skills or information as a result of playing the game.

- **Puzzles and trivia:** This category includes games like Sudoku, word search, or Trivial Pursuit.

- **Racing and flying:** These games involve cars, go-karts, snowboards, jet skis, biplanes, jets, or spacecraft competing with one another. The challenge in games within this genre is typically hand-eye coordination.

- **Shooting:** Shooting games involve — you guessed it — shooting. The projectiles can be anything from bullets to marshmallows to anti-ballistic missiles.

- **Sports and recreation:** These games are electronic interpretations of real-world activities that incorporate some of the skill or strategy elements of the original game. They vary based on the level of detail.

- **Fighting:** Fighting games — also called combat games — involve some kind of simulated physical battle. They vary based upon the level of gore.

- **Role playing:** In this genre, a game master creates an alternative world that encourages social interactions.

- **Strategy and simulation:** These games emphasize decision-making skills. The best-known decision-making board game, which also comes in electronic versions, is chess. This category includes a variety of games with varying levels of complexity and agreement with reality.

There are three levels of engagement in games:

- **Single player:** Single-player games pit you against the clock, your dexterity, chance, or the computer (playing as an imaginary competitor).

- **Multi-player games:** In these games, instead of playing against the computer, you play against friends, family, or even strangers.

✏ **Massively multi-player games:** Massively multi-player games involve the creation of a set of rules for an alternative society. The largest is World of Warcraft, which has over 10 million subscribers. But that's just one of the many games in this category. These games involve role playing, strategy, and simulation, but can involve shooting or other sports.

Just as there are ratings for the age appropriateness of movies, there are comparable ratings for video games. The ratings are about the level of challenge in the game, not about the amount of sex or violence.

Here's a key to what the rates mean:

✏ **eC:** Early childhood

✏ **E:** Everyone

✏ **E10+:** Everyone 10 years old or older

✏ **T:** Teenagers

✏ **M:** Mature

✏ **RP:** Rating pending

 Xbox LIVE has a policy that excludes very explicit adult material. Mature titles may be available for your phone, but they won't push the boundaries for most people.

Where to Buy Games

There are two sources of games for Windows Phone users:

✏ **The Internet:** Many Web sites offer games that are free or subscription supported. If your favorite Web-based game has a mobile version, it's already set up for you to use on your Windows Phone. If not, you'll become proficient at zooming and panning gestures! The good news is that you can keep up with your game while you're away from your PC.

✏ **Windows Phone Marketplace:** I describe how to get games from the Marketplace in Chapter 17.

My take on Microsoft's vision of gaming

Microsoft has its own take on how people can get the most out of gaming and, not surprisingly, it revolves around Microsoft platforms. Relying solely on Microsoft is not necessarily how most of us plan our entertainment. Fortunately, you can always play some games on the Internet.

Don't forget, though, that Microsoft does have some cool ideas that can benefit the gamer in you:

✔ **The development platform used for Xbox runs on the Windows Phone.** This does not mean that games that run on your Xbox can run on your phone — there are too many differences between the Xbox console and your phone. However, it does make it more convenient for game programmers to rework their code so the games are similar. That works in your favor.

✔ **Xbox LIVE is a unifying environment for gaming.** You don't need to register with Xbox LIVE to play games. However, doing so offers you a line of communication with like-minded gamers, including those who own the Xbox console, those on PCs, and Windows Phone 7 gamers. This adds a new dimension to multi-player games. (More on this in Chapter 18.)

Organized Fun on the Games Hub

The goal of the Games hub (shown in Figure 16-1) is to allow you to access your favorite games, whether you're seeking entertainment or you need to make a move in game.

Courtesy of Microsoft Corporation

Figure 16-1: The Windows Phone 7 Games hub in panorama.

Four screens are a part of the Game hub panorama:

- ✓ **Xbox LIVE:** This screen shows whether you're signed on to Xbox LIVE. As long as you're within cellular range, you're set.

  Also on this screen is your Xbox LIVE avatar. An *avatar* is a cartoon representation of your identity in the Xbox LIVE world. When you first come to this screen, you'll see a default avatar (like the one shown in Figure 16-2). Creating your own avatar is optional. However, some games — like Guitar Hero 5, Band Hero, and more — are more fun if you have a personalized avatar. To personalize your avatar, go to `http://marketplace.xbox.com/en-US/avatar/default.htm` and enter the gamertag that you created when you created your Windows Live ID; this is the same as your Zune Name (see Figure 16-3).

Figure 16-2: The avatar silhouette.

If you want to set up a personal avatar, be aware that many of the accessories involve using Microsoft points. Many of the options are free, but some customizations to your avatar cost money.

- ✓ **Requests:** Requests let you know when a game is waiting for you to take action. For example, you can be playing a game of chess on your Windows Phone with your friend who is sitting at a Friendly's Restaurant in Defiance, Ohio, using his Windows Phone. He has just engaged in the Budapest Gambit, having moved 1.d4 Nf6 2.c4 e5. You'll get a notification that it's your turn to move. This appears as a request.

If your opponent is engaging in the Budapest Gambit, it's most effective to engage in the "Indian Defense" with a move of d4 Nf6.

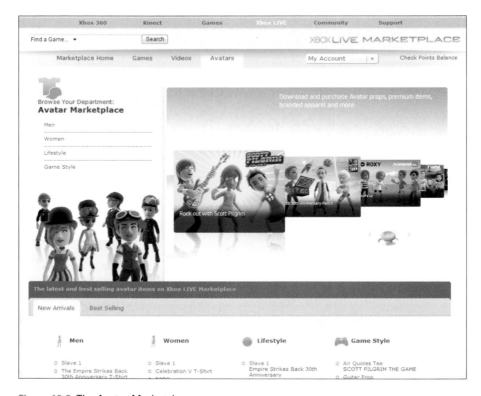

Figure 16-3: The Avatar Marketplace.

The point is that the Requests screen lets you know when any and all of your games are waiting for you to take a move. Having this appear in the Games hub avoids the problem of clogging up your e-mail or text inbox.

⊭ **Collection:** The Collection screen (shown in Figure 16-4) includes all the games that you have stored on your phone. When you first get your Windows Phone, your Collection screen is empty. But when you start adding games in Chapter 17, this screen is where you can launch the games that you own.

⊭ **Spotlight:** The Spotlight screen is a source of information on gaming. These are messages created by Microsoft to let you know new information and options about games. This includes new product releases and ways to improve your gaming experiences.

Courtesy of Microsoft Corporation

Figure 16-4: The Games Collection screen shows all your games.

Getting Games on Your Phone

In This Chapter

▶ Navigating the games available on the Marketplace

▶ Paying for games

▶ Downloading games to your phone

▶ Keeping track of what you've downloaded

*L*oading games on your phone offers several advantages:

✓ You don't have to be connected to the Internet to play.

✓ You get support from Xbox LIVE Marketplace (see Chapter 18).

✓ The game can use the capabilities of your Windows Phone to be more "immersive." For example, your phone has a multi-touch screen and sensors, such as the accelerometer and the GPS receiver. The accelerometer doesn't do much for trivia games, but it does make racing games that you can control by moving the phone much more interesting.

In this chapter, I tell you how to find the games you want on the Marketplace and how to keep track of what you've downloaded.

The Games Department of the Windows Phone Marketplace

The Marketplace is where you can buy games and other applications. The points that you prepay to get music files and applications (see Chapter 9) are the same points that you can use to acquire games on your phone.

Figure 17-1 shows the Marketplace hub. Tap the Games link, and that takes you to the Games section of the Marketplace. Alternatively, you can tap Marketplace from the Games hub (see Figure 17-2) and get to the same place.

All the rules that apply to Marketplace in general apply to the games section, including the following:

- You buy points once you enter your credit card or enter information from a gift card. You use these points for games or applications

- When you download the game, it confirms for you when it is ready to play.

- There is a seven-day, no-questions-asked return policy on your games.

- There may be other ways that the game manufacturer offers you a chance to learn about its games, such as entry-level games.

- Your games are verified each time you try to play them to ensure that they're valid.

- You may get notices of updates and revisions to games as they become available.

The games are organized into nine game genres (see Chapter 16). A game may appear in more than one genre.

Figure 17-1: The Marketplace hub.

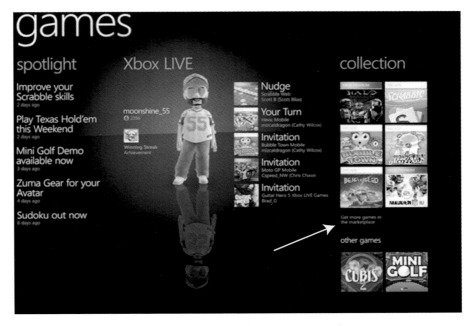

Figure 17-2: The Games hub with Marketplace highlighted.

When you're in a genre that looks promising, there are two ways narrow your choices among similar titles:

- **Ratings:** Gamers love to exalt good games and bash bad ones. Figure 17-3 shows a panorama of a game description. After the price is the star rating of the game. The star rating is displayed prominently because of its importance in helping you choose which games to buy.

- **Featured:** Another way to select games is to rely on featured games (see Figure 17-4).

The return policy on Marketplace allows you to return games that don't live up to your expectations. Don't be shy about using it! (For more on the return policy, turn to Chapter 9.)

Figure 17-3: A game description.

Figure 17-4: Featured games.

Keeping Track of the Games on Your Phone

All the games that you've acquired are available in the Games hub under the Games Collection (see Figure 17-5). Here, you see all the current games that are authorized to run on your phone. The tiles are sorted based on when you most recently used them. To begin playing a game, just tap on the tile and the game launches.

Figure 17-5: The Games Collection on your phone.

Xbox LIVE and Mobile

In This Chapter

▶ Introducing Xbox LIVE

▶ Accessing Xbox LIVE from your phone

Many games on mobile phones are self-contained entertainment applications. They can be incredibly sophisticated, but mostly you play against the computer.

The Windows Phone offers similar games, but it distinguishes itself from other smartphones primarily by integrating with Xbox LIVE. This chapter describes Xbox LIVE in more detail, explaining how you can access Xbox LIVE from your phone.

What Xbox LIVE Is

Windows Live is the central repository for games and gaming information that run on different Microsoft platforms. These have included the Xbox console and Windows-based PCs. Now Xbox LIVE includes games and gaming information that can run on Windows Phone 7.

Microsoft's situation is unique in that it is the only developer that offers games developers three platforms: the PC, a console (the Xbox), and a mobile environment. Microsoft's main competitors, Sony and Nintendo, can only offer a console and a mobile platform. The advantage of having a game run on multiple platforms is that you, as the gamer, can have a familiar experience where it's convenient for you.

One issue with having the same game on multiple platforms is keeping straight your highest score. Xbox LIVE takes care of that detail. After you've connected all your platforms on Xbox LIVE, there is the added benefit of sharing hints for that game, learning about other games that may be of interest, and having a messaging platform that you use exclusively for gaming information.

This last option warrants more discussion. On the one hand, it's convenient to get all your messages at one address. On the other hand, many gamers find that it works best to keep their gaming communications separate from either their work or their personal e-mail. You may find it annoying to be prodded to make your next game move on the same e-mail account where you get other messages. The good news with Xbox LIVE and its integration with Windows Phone is that you can set up your communications either way you like it: Combining your gaming communications via Xbox LIVE or keeping it separate.

Some of what you find on Xbox LIVE is free, but you have to pay for the rest. There are two levels of access, Silver and Gold, which determine the range of services that are available to you. By virtue of your having a Windows Live ID, you are automatically at the Silver level. There is no charge for this level. Read on for more information.

The free stuff

The Silver membership comes with your Windows Live ID. This is a basic level of service where you can manage your avatar. It also lets you store and compare your score for what Xbox LIVE calls Arcade games (essentially, single-player games where you play against the machine — as opposed to multi-player games where you play against another person).

Through the Xbox LIVE on your PC, you can look at the Xbox LIVE Marketplace. Of course, anything you would want to buy costs money, but access to the Marketplace is free.

In the Xbox LIVE Marketplace, you see which games work on which platforms (PC, Xbox console, or Windows Phone). When you come to Marketplace through your Windows Phone, its default setting is to show you only the games that you can use with your phone.

The not-free stuff

There is also the option to upgrade to the Gold level. The Gold membership offers you two capabilities that you can't get with a Silver membership:

- Support for multi-player games
- Messaging

A Gold membership for Xbox LIVE currently costs $7.99 per month on a monthly basis. There are discounts if you commit to extended periods, such as $49.99 for 12 months.

This pricing is subject to change. It's also subject to promotions and introductory deals. If you're unsure whether Xbox LIVE Gold membership is for you, be sure to find out whether you can save money on your membership.

Figure 18-1 shows the Xbox LIVE home screen (www.xbox.com) available on your PC.

Figure 18-1: Gold-level membership on the PC version of Xbox LIVE.

Signing up for a membership starts by clicking on the link to get a Gold membership. You'll be prompted to select a payment option.

Multi-player games

As the name implies, a multi-player game allows you to compete against other players. These games fall into two categories:

✔ **Turn-by-turn multi-player games:** Turn-by-turn games are similar to chess. Once you make a move, it's your competitor's turn to respond. She could respond in just a few seconds, or should take minutes or even hours to respond.

✔ **Real-time games:** Real-time games are faster than turn-by-turn ones. Tennis is a real-time game — you hit the ball and in just a few seconds, your opponent hits the ball back. She can't wait to hit the ball until she gets back from running errands.

The Windows Phone supports only turn-by-turn multi-player games. A real-time game requires reliable broadband. You can get that on a PC or an Xbox console, but your Windows Phone isn't quite there yet.

Messaging

Messaging through the Xbox is more than just another way to communicate with your friends through a different server. The special kinds of messages that relate to gaming include

✔ Move requests and updates

✔ Hints and requests for hints

✔ Game status updates

✔ Game suggestions

E-mail, message boards, and instant messaging services are not as convenient as the specialized services on Xbox Message. Plus, through Xbox Message, you can get periodic updates on game-related information, such as notifications on seminars to improve your game skills or announcements of new promotions.

There are two categories of messages:

✔ **Requests:** Requests are messages that ask you to take action. For example, a request lets you know that your competitor has taken action since your last move, and now it's your turn.

✔ **Spotlight:** Spotlight messages contain information on upcoming sessions and webinars related to gaming area that you've opted into.

Xbox LIVE from Your Windows Phone

To access Xbox LIVE on your phone, tap the Xbox LIVE tile on the Start screen (see Figure 18-2). You'll be taken to the Games hub (shown in Figure 18-3).

The leftmost part of the Games hub is the Spotlight. Figure 18-4 shows a sample of the messages included in Spotlight. Spotlight messages are useful, but not as urgent as Requests (see Figure 18-5); requests are messages that tell you that a competitor has made a move and that it's your turn to take the next step.

Figure 18-2: The Xbox LIVE tile on the Start screen.

Figure 18-3: The Windows Phone 7 Games hub in panorama.

You can pan over to the right and get to your Games Collection, where you can open up the game. Otherwise, your competitor will just need to wait until you get to your PC or Xbox console. In the meantime, you'll have information about your competitor's move so that you can begin considering your next steps.

It shouldn't be a surprise that you can send and not just receive messages from your Windows Phone. In addition to the automated messages you receive, you can write a message to another person as long as you know their Gamertag.

Figure 18-4: Xbox LIVE Spotlight messages.

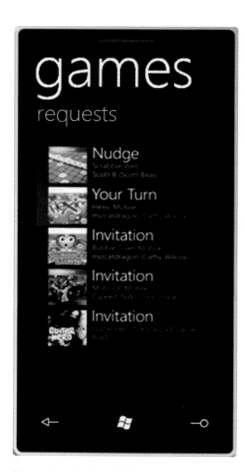

Figure 18-5: An Xbox LIVE request.

Part VII

Taking Care of Business with Your Windows Phone

The 5th Wave   By Rich Tennant

"Jim and I do a lot of business together on Facebook. By the way, Jim, did you get the sales spreadsheet and little blue pony I sent you?"

In this part . . .

Among the most commonly used tools in most business environments is your electronic calendar. In this part, I tell you how to make additions, changes, and deletions to your electronic business calendar from your Windows Phone. I also explain how to merge your personal calendar with your business calendar, so the right level of information is shared with each. This flexibility ensures that you can keep control of the semi-personal/semi-business activities that take place during business hours, while avoiding scheduling conflicts.

Sure, you can have a lot of fun with your Windows Phone . . . but you can get a lot done with it, too, and in this part, I show you how.

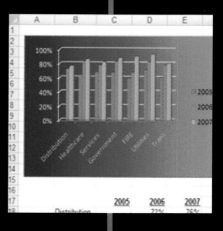

19

On the Road Again: Taking Your Work with You on Your Phone

In This Chapter

▶ Using Mobile Office applications

▶ Navigating the Office hub on your phone

▶ Sharing files on your phone

Microsoft puts Office Mobile on your phone, which means you can work with Microsoft Office applications when on the road without the need to pull out your laptop. Depending on what you want to do, you may even be able to leave your heavy laptop at home.

The Windows Phone doesn't allow you to leave computers behind for good. The size of the screen and the keyboard aren't conducive for writing novels and other similarly long documents.

In this chapter, I introduce you to the Office apps on your phone and explain how you can use them to your best advantage. Then I walk you through the Office hub, so you know where everything is. Finally, I fill you in on file sharing, so you can get files off your phone and out into the world.

Mobile Office Apps

The Office applications on your Windows Phone can allow you to be very productive on the road, without a laptop. The following Microsoft Office applications are on your Windows Phone:

- **Classic Microsoft Office applications:** These are the Office applications in use by most businesses and many consumers on their PCs:

  - **Microsoft Word Mobile:** For creating and editing documents

  - **Microsoft Excel Mobile:** For managing spreadsheets, performing numerical analysis, and creating charts

  - **Microsoft PowerPoint Mobile:** For viewing presentations

- **Microsoft OneNote:** A newer addition to the Microsoft Office family. As the name implies, it's intended as a tool for you to take fast and accurate notes. It also allows you to embed sound recordings. It doesn't have the fancy tools to create pretty or formal documents. It does allow you to type in your thoughts, add graphics and sound files, and rearrange them as you organize your thoughts. Then it's set up to allow you to reformat your work back into the Classic Microsoft Office applications.

- **Microsoft SharePoint:** This is the client side of the Microsoft SharePoint Server. It's a collaboration tool to help multiple people share and edit files at the same time.

The issue of file sharing is integral to getting the most out of the Office applications on your phone. The most basic scenario is one in which you're working on a Microsoft Office file yourself. If you have a desktop PC, you're probably accustomed to transferring that file among different machines if you want to work on it in different locations. Here are your options:

- **Thumb drive:** In this scenario, you use a thumb drive to move the file from one PC to another. The only problem here is that your Windows Phone doesn't have a USB port to plug the thumb drive into.

- **E-mail:** In this scenario, you e-mail the file from one PC to another.

- **Server:** In this scenario, you save a copy of your file from the first PC on a remote server that you can access from both the first and second PC.

In each of these scenarios, you take personal responsibility to ensure that you're revising the latest (or correct) version of the file and that you've stored the latest version of the file back to the original PC. Managing revisions of files is hard enough by yourself, but when many people are working on the same document, the challenge grows exponentially.

To solve this problem, Microsoft came up with SharePoint. If your company uses SharePoint, you're set. If it doesn't, you can skip the coverage of SharePoint in this book.

My take on Microsoft's vision of Office productivity

Here's my slightly cynical inference of how Microsoft wants you to use the Mobile Office applications:

- **Use OneNote as the primary tool for entering information into Microsoft Office format.** Collect your creative thoughts, your observations, and other input and enter it on to OneNote on your phone. Take the files that you create in this format, and move it to your desktop or laptop PC. Either keep these files as OneNote files or use them as necessary and appropriate in a more formal Office document.

- **Use the Mobile versions of Word, Excel, and PowerPoint to review files that were created on a laptop or desktop PC.** You also can make minor edits, customize revisions, or make comments.

- **Use SharePoint to practice revision control.** If your company doesn't have SharePoint, put pressure on the Information Technology (IT) department within your organization to get on the ball and get it. If you're a senior executive in your firm, insist that your IT department get SharePoint, the same way other executives pressured their organizations to support the iPhone a few years ago.

- **If you don't have SharePoint, you can use the e-mail or server method of sharing files.** Good luck with the revision control. Don't say I didn't warn you.

Office Hub on Your Phone

The Office hub on your phone (shown in Figure 19-1) has four screens:

Figure 19-1: The Microsoft Office hub.

✓ **OneNote:** Includes tiles for recent OneNote documents

✓ **Documents:** Shorthand for "Recent Documents" for Word, Excel, and PowerPoint

✓ **SharePoint:** Has recent information on files recently uploaded or downloaded

✓ **Links:** Optional links that you set up to connect to Office files on servers or the Internet

OneNote

As mentioned previously, Microsoft's intent is to direct you to using OneNote for most of your Mobile Office work. OneNote is the first screen on the Office hub. It also uses tiles to make it that much easier for you to tap and bring up a OneNote page (as shown in Figure 19-2).

The use of "note taking" software is not nearly as widespread in the rest of the world as it is in Redmond, Washington (where Microsoft is based). OneNote seems to be the runaway favorite for note taking in that town as well.

At the same time, relying on OneNote for most office applications does make sense on the phone. This application is built for flexibility, which makes its use in this application more appropriate than the classic Office applications for basic information collection.

Also, the power of the Classic Office applications is in the myriad of ways you can format a document just the way you want, manage multiple spreadsheets simultaneously, and present information to large groups. Your Windows Phone is not set up for these roles.

Think of OneNote as a binder of paper, where you can add

✓ Typed-in text

✓ Images

✓ Sound recordings

✓ Hyperlinks to Web sites

✓ Movies

✓ Charts

Courtesy of Microsoft Corporation

Figure 19-2: The OneNote home screen.

In each case, you start with a blank electronic sheet of paper. In this sense, it is most similar to when you open a new Word document. You get the blank sheet when you tap on the plus sign and open a OneNote page. In fact, when you start typing, you may not be able to tell any difference between Mobile Word and Mobile OneNote; the differences are more apparent when you work with the other formats.

Documents

The Documents screen is for the Classic Office applications and the files that you've created. At first, you'll see the names of these applications on the screen (as shown in Figure 19-3). After you've worked with and saved some files on your phone, they'll be available on this screen.

If you want more information about Microsoft Office, check out *Microsoft Office 2007 For Dummies,* by Wallace Wang (published by Wiley).

In general, the mobile versions of the Office applications can work with complex documents that you've downloaded to your phone. However, you can't access all the nuances within the application available on the PC versions.

Figure 19-3: The Documents screen.

In addition, the Mobile Office applications may not have the fonts that you're using in the PC versions. Not to worry — the Mobile Office applications substitute similar fonts so that you can continue to work.

The formatting of the document on your phone may not be exactly the same as it is when it reappears on your PC. Save yourself time and don't try to format a document on your Windows Phone.

Microsoft Word Mobile

The ultimate output of this application is a printed document. You can't connect a printer to your Windows Phone. This highlights the role of Word Mobile as an accessory to a PC and, more specifically, a PC that has a printer.

At the same time, you can type into a new or an existing document. The process involves a very limited number of the standard Word commands, including:

✔ New

✔ Open

✔ Save

✔ Send

✔ Comment

✔ Font customizations, including

- A limited range of font types
- Color
- Italics
- Underline

The image in Figure 19-4 shows what the screen looks like.

Microsoft Excel Mobile

More than the other classic mobile office application, your satisfaction with using Excel Mobile depends on your ambitions. A new spreadsheet is shown in Figure 19-5.

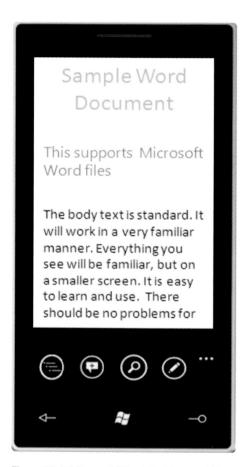

Figure 19-4: Microsoft Word Mobile on a Windows Phone.

As you can see, there is room for only 52 cells. This compares to a PC with an LCD screen that shows between 1,000 and 2,000 cells. Still, Excel Mobile can analyze the data on the sheet. As shown in Figure 19-6, it can present you with detailed charts.

As long as your needs involve reviewing the work of others and making minor updates, you should be happy.

Figure 19-5: A new spreadsheet on Excel Mobile.

Microsoft PowerPoint Mobile

PowerPoint Mobile is good for reviewing existing presentations and making edits. Because it doesn't have an external display option, the screen on the phone won't make for a good presentation tool unless you're really desperate and all else has gone wrong.

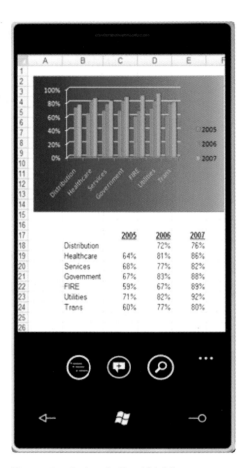

Figure 19-6: A chart in Excel Mobile.

With that warning, the image on Figure 19-7 shows a title screen and the first page of a PowerPoint presentation.

With the font substitutions, the screen displays presentations reasonably well, unless the presentation has a large amount of writing. The mobile app does best when the presentation slides are graphics intensive.

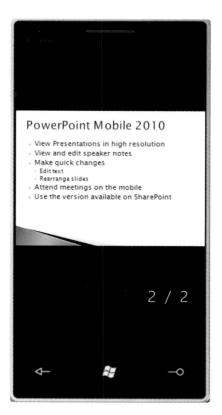

Figure 19-7: PowerPoint Mobile on the Windows Phone.

SharePoint

SharePoint is a powerful tool that enables companies to manage revision control among multiple employees.

If your employer doesn't have a SharePoint Server, and you have no influence on whether the company does get one, just skip this section and ignore the SharePoint screen on your phone.

If your employer already has a SharePoint Server, you need to work with the company to set up permissions for your phone. There are three levels of access to a document on a SharePoint Server:

- Read and write access
- Read-only access
- No access

These permissions are set up by the folder administrator. When you download a given document, the system automatically tracks your changes, just as it does when you're on your desktop or laptop PC. Although you have fewer controls with your Office Mobile applications, SharePoint is happy to track what you have.

Links

This screen doesn't have a title, but by tapping the Add Links icon, you can add a permanent, or semipermanent, link to a document that you'd like to more easily download. This makes accessing a document from SharePoint, a remote server, or a Web site as easy at tapping on it. To make this work, follow these steps from the Office hub:

1. **Drag the hub screen to the far right where you see the plus sign that says Add Links, and tap that link.**

   A screen appears asking you for the following:

   - **Title:** A name that you want to use
   - **Source:** For example, the Web site or SharePoint
   - **Document location:** The location on the drive or the Internet address

2. **Enter all this information, and tap Done.**

   This link appears in your list of links.

File Sharing outside of SharePoint

Other than using SharePoint (see "SharePoint," earlier), you can send or receive Office files with your phone in two ways: e-mail or a shared server.

Using e-mail to review and edit files

In this scenario, you either e-mail the file to yourself from your personal PC or someone else e-mails it to you from his PC. This e-mail, with the attached file, shows up on your phone. From there, follow these steps:

1. **Tap the e-mail with the attachment.**

   This opens the message.

2. **Tap the attachment.**

   It asks if you want to:

   - Save the file
   - Open the file
   - Cancel and return to reading the e-mail

3. **Tap the option to save the file.**

   The file appears under documents on your Office hub.

4. **Close the e-mail.**

5. **Close the e-mail application.**

6. **Press the Start button to get to the Start screen.**

7. **Tap on the Office tile on the Start screen.**

8. **Move one screen to the right to get to the Documents screen on the Office hub.**

   Your saved document is the first one.

9. **Tap your document to open it.**

10. **Read it and/or make edits and comments.**

11. **To save it, tap the ellipsis at the bottom-right corner of the screen, and tap Save.**

12. **To e-mail the document back to yourself (for your PC) or to the person who wanted your comments, tap the ellipsis again, and tap Send.**

    This automatically attaches the document to an e-mail.

13. **Enter the name of the person to whom you want to send the document in the To field.**

14. **Tap Send.**

    The updated document is sent to the intended recipient.

Using SkyDrive or another remote server

These days, the cost of hard drives is miniscule. Different organizations are willing to offer you shared server space for next to nothing or for free. For example, simply by virtue of having a Windows Live ID, Microsoft lets you store up to 25 GB of data for free on SkyDrive (`http://skydrive.live.com`).

Dozens of other companies offer a similar service, usually for drive backup. I'll use SkyDrive to describe how to make this kind of service a convenience for use with your Windows Phone.

1. **Save the desired file on your PC to SkyDrive.**

   See Figure 19-8 for how the file folder looks on your PC.

Figure 19-8: SkyDrive folders.

2. Click the Personal folder.

You see the screen shown in Figure 19-9.

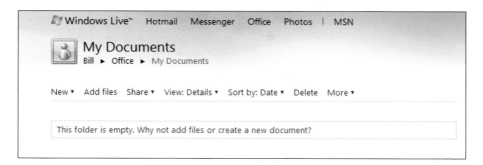

Figure 19-9: Your personal SkyDrive folder.

3. Click the Add Files link.

This brings you to Figure 19-10.

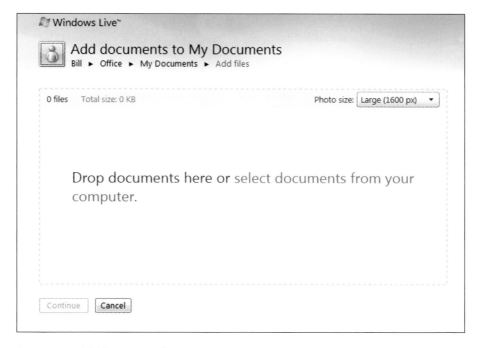

Figure 19-10: Add files to your SkyDrive folder.

4. **Drag the file that you want to edit onto the box.**

   The file starts uploading to SkyDrive. It lets you know when it's done and asks whether you want to add any more (as shown in Figure 19-11). When the answer is no, you can close SkyDrive.

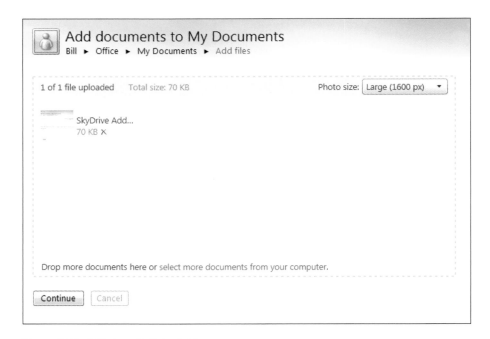

Add documents to My Documents
Bill ► Office ► My Documents ► Add files

1 of 1 file uploaded   Total size: 70 KB   Photo size: [Large (1600 px) ▼]

SkyDrive Add...
70 KB ✗

Drop more documents here or select more documents from your computer.

[Continue] [Cancel]

Figure 19-11: A file in a SkyDrive folder.

If you want someone else to be able to send you files, you can have her put a file into your public folder. You determine who has access to your SkyDrive.

Accessing the file from your Windows Phone involves using your Web browser. Go to `http://skydrive.live.com` to get the file you just saved.

In theory, you can open the file from SkyDrive, edit it, and then save it back to SkyDrive. The problem is: What happens if you lose connectivity when you're working on the file? Word Mobile gets confused and upset. It's more reliable to save the file to your phone, edit it, save the updated file to your phone again, and then save back to SkyDrive:

1. **Save the file to your phone by opening your Internet browser on your Start screen and going to** `http://skydrive.live.com`**.**

2. **When you see the file you want, tap it.**

   SkyDrive gives you the option to

   - Save the file

   - Open the file

   - Cancel and return to reading the e-mail

3. **Save the file to your phone.**

   It appears on the Document screen in your Office hub.

4. **Close the e-mail.**

5. **Close the e-mail application.**

6. **Press the Start button to get to the Start screen.**

7. **Tap the Office tile on the Start screen.**

8. **Move one screen to the right to get to the Documents screen on the Office hub.**

   Your saved document is the first one.

9. **Tap the document to open it.**

10. **Read it and/or make edits and comments.**

11. **To save the document, tap the ellipsis at the bottom-right corner of the screen and tap Save.**

12. **To move it back to SkyDrive, close out of Office Mobile, and press the Start button to get to the Start screen.**

13. **Return to SkyDrive on your phone's Internet browser.**

14. **Save the updated file back to your SkyDrive.**

    It makes sense to overwrite the old file to avoid confusion.

15. **When you return to your PC, the file will be ready for you.**

20

Making a Date with Your Phone

In This Chapter

▶ Setting up appointments

▶ Downloading your calendars to your phone

▶ Uploading appointments to your PC

*Y*ou may fall in love with your Windows Phone so much that you want to ask it out on a date, but the subject of this chapter is the calendar on your phone. The Windows Phone calendar functions are cool and powerful, and they can make your life easier. With just a few taps, you can bring all your electronic calendars together to keep your life synchronized.

I start the chapter by showing you how to set up the stand-alone calendar on your phone (without synchronizing with other calendars). Then I show you how to integrate all your electronic calendars with your Windows Phone. After you read this chapter, you'll have no excuse for missing a meeting.

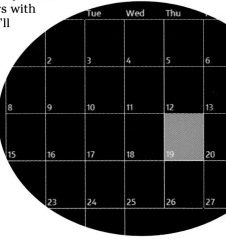

Stand-Alone with Me: Setting Up Your Phone's Calendar

Your Windows Phone has a Calendar app that comes in very handy. In this section, I show you how to set your date format preferences, how to access the Calendar itself, and how to make an appointment in your Calendar app.

Setting your date and time preferences

To make changes in your date and time settings, follow these steps:

1. **From the Start screen, pan one screen to the right to get to the applications list.**

2. **Flick down to the Settings application icon, shown in Figure 20-1.**

3. **Tap Settings.**

   The General settings screen (shown in Figure 20-2) appears.

Figure 20-1: The Settings icon within the applications list.

Figure 20-2: The General settings.

4. **Flick down to get to Date and Time, and tap that link.**

   Tapping the option you want to change allows you to make the changes to the following settings:

   - 12-hour or 24-hour clock

   - What day is considered the first day of the week (see Figure 20-3)

   - Which of the multiple options you prefer for presenting the date (see Figure 20-4 for a sample)

Figure 20-3: Your First Day of Week options in Date and Time settings.

Set your preferences, and all the applications on the phone are updated accordingly.

Figure 20-4: Date presentation options in Date and Time settings.

Getting to the Calendar

The default Calendar is on your Start screen. It has a large tile with the current date (shown in Figure 20-5). To start the Calendar app, tap the Calendar tile. This brings you to a small panorama with two screen options:

✔ **Day:** This option (see Figure 20-6) shows your daily calendar with the times that already have appointments blocked out. The amount of time between appointments is clearly open.

✔ **Agenda:** This option (see Figure 20-7) shows a chronological listing of all your appointments.

What about your monthly calendar? As long as you don't have too many appointments, this view may be helpful. To judge for yourself, tap the Monthly Calendar icon on the Daily screen. Figure 20-8 shows the Monthly Calendar icon and a sample of how the monthly calendar looks.

Courtesy of Microsoft Corporation

Figure 20-5: The Calendar tile on the Start screen.

Figure 20-6: The Day calendar screen.

Making a new appointment

Before you make a new appointment, you need to have the following information at hand:

- ✔ **Subject:** This is what you want to name the appointment. Call it whatever helps you remember what it is (such as "Coffee with Joe").

- ✔ **Location:** This is a text box where you enter the location of your meeting. This field can be left blank.

✔ **Account:** For this section of the chapter, I'm just using the option "DeviceStore" for the stand-alone calendar. I explore the other options in the next section.

✔ **When:** There are two entry fields — one is for the date, and the other is for the start time.

✔ **How Long:** This is the duration of the meeting.

Figure 20-7: The Agenda calendar screen.

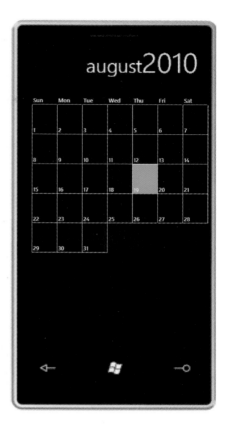

Figure 20-8: The monthly calendar option.

If you want, you can enter more details on the meeting:

✓ **Reminder:** If you select this option, your phone gives you a warning of an upcoming meeting a few minutes before it's to take place (see Figure 20-9). The default is for the reminder to pop up at the start time of the meeting, but you can set it to appear before the meeting takes place, giving yourself some time to get there.

✓ **Occurs:** Some meetings take place only one time. The default option is Once. If this is a recurring meeting, you can set it up so that you don't have to reenter the meeting every day, week, month, and so on.

Figure 20-9: Calendar pop-up alerting you to a meeting.

✔ **Status:** If you're on a calendar that other people can access, it can be useful to define your degree of confidence in that meeting's time setting. Here are the different options:

- **Busy:** This is the most typical status. You use it when you know that you have a firm time set aside that no one else can access unless you change the current appointment.

- **Tentative:** This the electronic version of penciling in an appointment. It reminds you that the meeting hasn't been set firmly.

- **Out of the Office:** This option is useful when you're on vacation or traveling.

- **Free:** Sometimes you want to keep your options open by putting in a placeholder for a meeting. If you use the Free status, you can schedule an appointment at the same time.

✔ **Attendees:** This option reminds you who will be present at the meeting.

✔ **Notes:** This is free space for you to write notes for yourself about this meeting.

To add an appointment, follow these steps:

1. **Tap the plus icon on the Daily screen.**

   This brings up the screen shown in Figure 20-10.

Figure 20-10: The New Appointment screen.

2. **Enter the information described earlier.**

3. **Either tap Done or tap More Information. If you tap More Information, go ahead and add it. Then tap Done when you're, well, done.**

   The appointment is added automatically to your calendar, which is also visible on your list of appointments.

Your Calendars Together at Last

As promised, you can add all your electronic calendars to your phone, which gives you a view into your entire schedule.

You may have a work calendar and a personal calendar. And you may be reluctant to put your personal calendar on your work calendar for your colleagues to see. A Windows Phone lets you integrate all the calendars, but keep them independent.

Linking your electronic calendars to your phone

The first step is to link to your electronic calendars. To set up your calendar to synch with your phone, follow the steps in Chapter 11 for setting up your e-mail account. When you set up an e-mail account, the default is for your calendar to synch with your phone automatically. If you've already set up your e-mail and your calendar hasn't synched, this is usually because you were offered the option to do this when you set up your e-mail account, but, for some reason, this selection was unchecked.

To address this problem, repeat the process of adding an e-mail account covered in Chapter 11. If your e-mail service offers you the choice of synchronizing different services — which can include e-mail, notes, contacts, and either appointments or a calendar — make sure that all are checked.

If you're using an electronic calendar that is associated with an e-mail service that isn't on the supported list (see Chapter 11), the setup process is also beyond the scope of this book. The Windows Phone uses Microsoft's Exchange ActiveSync service, which is a common industry standard. However, it is not universal. Your best option would be to try using the calendar on Windows Live and integrate it there.

Creating an appointment for one calendar

Figure 20-10, earlier in this chapter, has an entry for Account. I used DeviceStore for my stand-alone calendar, but now I have multiple calendars synchronizing with my phone, each associated with an e-mail account.

You may already be a winner!

The calendar on your phone may already be populated with appointments from your work and personal e-mail accounts. Don't be concerned — this is good news!

What happened is that, back in Chapter 11, you set up your phone to link to your e-mail. You used the Add an Account screen, shown here. And you may have been presented with the option to synchronize your calendar along with your e-mail (this is the default option). If so, you're all done — your calendars are synchronizing with your phone.

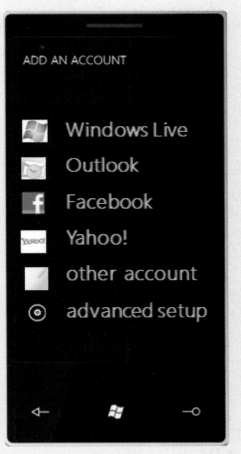

To save a new appointment to the correct calendar, you simply select which account you want. The phone updates the appropriate calendar automatically.

To ensure that you update the correct calendar, you have the option to assign a unique color code to the appointments associated with the different calendars. Here's how, starting from the Daily screen:

1. **Tap the Ellipsis at the bottom-right corner.**

2. **Tap Manage Accounts.**

    The screen shown in Figure 20-11 appears.

    By default, all the calendars have the same color.

3. **To change the color of a calendar, tap where it says Auto (or another color name, if you've already changed the color before).**

    This brings you to a screen shown in Figure 20-12.

Figure 20-11: The color assignment screen for calendars.

4. Tap the color you want and then tap Done.

All the appointments from that calendar will now be that color.

Figure 20-12: Your color options.

Part VIII
The Part of Tens

The 5th Wave — By Rich Tennant

"Russell! Do you remember last month when I told you to order 150 SMART phones for the sales department?"

In this part . . .

When you're short on time, and you still want a lot of bang for your buck, this is the part for you.

Here, you find ten (or so) steps to making your Windows Phone your very own — everything from customizing your customizing your Start screen to customizing your color scheme and more.

I also fill you in on ten features the Windows Phone should and may have someday — from a compass to cut and paste. Your Windows Phone is great, but it can be even better, and in this part, I explain how.

eople

 Shai Bassli

edit

pin to start

delete

XBOX
LIVE
Games

Clock

23
Calendar

Calculator

 Marketplace

 Messaging

 OneNote

 People

 Pictures

 PowerPoint

Settings

Ten (Or So) Steps to Making the Phone Totally Yours

A cellphone is a very personal device. From the moment you take it out of the box and strip off the packaging, you begin to make it yours. By the end of the first day, even though millions of your type of phone may have been sold, there was no other phone just like yours.

This is the case not only because of the phone calls you make, but because of all the options that you can set on the phone. This is truer for the Windows Phone than any other phone available today. The exceptional access to social networking sites, the applications that you can download, and the Windows Live services, just to name a few, allow you to customize the phone more than any other phone on the market.

In this chapter, I cover numerous ways you can customize your phone.

Population Explosion: Adding Your Contacts

You can add contacts to your phone in several ways:

- Add them when they call, text, or e-mail you.
- Create contacts on your phone or PC.
- Call them and then add them to your contacts.
- Import them from your Windows Live e-mail and contacts list.
- Import them from your social networking sites.

With just a little bit of effort and the use of the tools that Windows Live offers, you can keep all your contacts organized and avoid out of date or duplicate information.

You Look Marvelous: Putting Up Custom Screen Images

Most cellphone users take a ton of pictures with their phones . . . and then let them sit there forever. But the Windows Phone gives you many tools to make it easy to download your photos and link them to your contacts. You can also use any of the pictures on your phone to put on your Start screen. More information on this subject is in Chapter 14.

Songs That Make the Whole World Sing: Downloading Your Music

Your music preferences are personal and unique. You can make your phone like no one else's with the music you have on it. For more information on playing music on your phone, turn to Chapter 14.

Making a Statement with Accessories

The Windows Phone is durable, but there are limits to how much abuse it can take. My advice: Get a case and/or wrapping (such as those you find on www. skinit.com) that protects your phone from damage. And with so many cases on the market, you can use yours to make a fashion statement, if that's your thing.

In Chapter 15, I pooh-pooh the notion of using a headset cord to connect your Windows Phone to a stereo. If you find HD radio as cool as I think you will, this'll sound better than your non-HD radio tuner when you play music through your stereo.

Chapter 1 covered how to connect Bluetooth headsets. There are lots of options these days for both single-earpiece and stereo-Bluetooth headsets, which make your phone experience more convenient and enjoyable.

Customizing Your Start Screen

The Start screen (see Chapter 1) is where you'll start from to get to most applications (hence, the name of the screen). When you get your phone out of the box, your Start screen will have a number of tiles for you to use. But you're not stuck with what's on your Start screen when you buy your phone. You have complete control over what is — or isn't — on this screen, as well as how the tiles are arranged. You can adorn your Start screen with contacts, Web pages, games, networking sites, and more.

Adding, moving, and deleting tiles on your Start screen is easy. You just follow a few simple steps. To add a tile:

1. **Find the application, game, or contact that you want to have on your Start screen.**

2. **With a finger, press and hold on its icon.**

   An option menu pops up (se Figure 21-1).

3. **Tap Pin to Start.**

   The item now appears at the bottom of the tiles on your Start screen.

When you add a tile, it's put at the bottom of the list, but this may not be where you want it. You can easily move around tiles by pressing on the tile and dragging it to where you want it in the list.

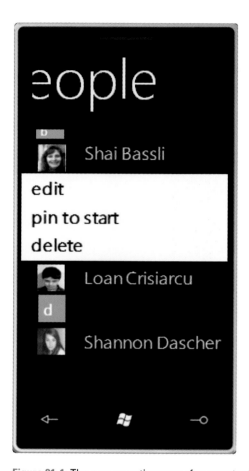

Figure 21-1: The pop-up option menu for a contact.

To remove a tile from the Start screen:

1. **Press and hold the tile you want to remove.**

   The unpin icon (shown in Figure 21-2) appears.

2. **Tap the unpin icon.**

   The tile is removed from the Start screen.

Figure 21-2: The unpin icon on a Start screen tile.

Removing the tile from your Start screen will not delete the application, game, or contact. If you want to delete it, you'll need to find the contact in your contacts file, the application on the application list next to the Start screen, or the game in your Games hub, and remove it there.

Setting Screen Colors

The Windows Phone allows you to control the background and the highlighted links on the screen.

The first option you have is to set the screen to be Dark or Light. Your phone uses much less battery power if it's set to the Dark mode.

The second option is to set the highlighting color, which can be orange, blue, red, green, or some other colors. The highlight color appears on links that you use to navigate around the phone, as well as on some of the tiles on the Start screen.

Here's how to change your screen colors:

1. **From the Start screen, pan one screen to the right to get to the applications list.**

2. **Flick down to the application icon for Settings, as shown in Figure 21-3.**

Figure 21-3: The Settings icon within the applications list.

3. **Tap Settings.**

   The screen shown in Figure 21-4 appears.

4. **Flick down to get to Theme and tap that link.**

   The screen shown in Figure 21-5 appears.

5. **Tap Background to set the background to either Light or Dark.**

6. **Tap Accent Color to set the color of the active links and some tiles.**

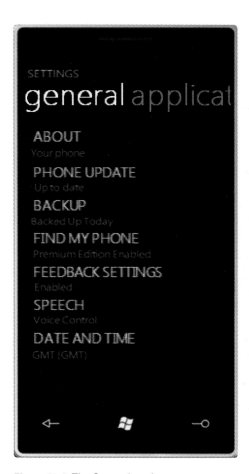

Figure 21-4: The General settings.

Figure 21-5: The Theme settings used to set colors.

Setting Your Password

Setting a password is strongly advised if you care at all about the information on your phone. Don't think you have anything on your phone that's very important? What about the names and addresses of everyone you know? Where you live? Your upcoming appointments (when you'll be away from home with an empty house just waiting to be looted)? Your financial information? All these are commonly found on people's cellphones, and if you lose your phone, a less-than-honorable person could wreak havoc with it.

Sure, having to tap in a four-digit numeric code every time you want to use your phone is slightly inconvenient. But if you lose your phone, you'll be glad it has a password.

Here's how to set your password:

1. **From the Start screen, pan one screen to the right to get to the applications list.**

2. **Flick down to the application icon for Settings and tap it.**

3. **Under General settings, tap Phone Lock.**

   The screen shown in Figure 21-6 appears.

Figure 21-6: The Lock screen.

4. **To turn on the password protection, tap to the right of the bar on the toggle switch that currently says Off.**

   It switches to On and asks you to enter a four-digit password.

5. **Tap in a four-digit password and tap Done.**

   Now you'll be asked to type this password each time you want to use your phone. It may be awkward at first, but you'll become adept at this quickly.

Signing Up for Microsoft's My Phone Service

Microsoft's My Phone service is an added form of security. The basic protection includes

- ✒ Backup and restoration service up to 200 MB of free online storage. This is more than enough space for all the information on your phone *other than* your photos, music, videos, and applications. ***Remember:*** Photos, music, and so on are available to be reloaded on your phone from Marketplace and Windows Live services.

- ✒ A map of the last known location of your phone based on the last synch or last photo share.

Your Windows Live ID does many of the same functions as the free My Phone. The Back Up and Restore service automates this process if you've lost your phone or otherwise need to switch to a new phone.

For what Microsoft calls a "nominal" fee, you can sign up for premium service. The premium service adds these capabilities:

- ✒ **Remote Ring:** This feature rings the phone on its loudest setting for up to one minute, even if you had the ringer set to silent or vibrate-only.

- ✒ **Remote Lock:** This allows you to create a four-digit pin (if you ignored the advice in the preceding section). You can also have the home screen display a message like "If found, please call 212-555-1212."

Remote Lock only works if you can get to a PC to add the password before someone accesses all the stuff on your phone that you don't want other people to access. In other words, you're always better off having a password on your phone all the time, instead of hoping you can set a Remote Lock before someone finds your phone.

✔ **Map Current Location:** This allows you to track, within the accuracy of the GPS signal, the location of your phone at the current moment (not just the last time you synched or did a photo share).

This option works best if you aren't sure if you left your phone when traveling, such as in the taxi or at the security checkpoint. If you know your phone is in your house, the accuracy of GPS isn't fine enough to tell you if it's lost between the seat cushions of your couch or in the pocket of your raincoat. But that's where the Remote Ring feature comes in handy.

 If you know that your phone was stolen and not just lost, do *not* try to track down the thief yourself. Get the police involved and let them know that you have this service on your phone and that you know where your phone is.

✔ **Remote Erase:** This option resets the phone to its factory settings, wiping out all the information and settings on your phone.

 You can't add the premium service after you've lost your phone. You must sign up for premium service beforehand.

Ten Features to Look for Down the Road

*I*f the capabilities of the Windows Phone in its initial release have only whetted your appetite and you want the phone to do more and more, this chapter is for you. Here, I get out my crystal ball and predict the kinds of things that Microsoft and its partners will be adding to the Windows Phone. I also describe some things that Windows Phones *should* be able to do — even if the chances of that happening are slim.

More and More Applications

The number of applications available to be downloaded on a smartphone has become a source of competitive advertising among the different platforms. More important is the breadth of applications. Either way, you can count on the fact that, however many applications exist now, there will be more within a few days. And they'll just keep on comin'.

All kinds of companies have made piles of money writing applications for PCs based on Microsoft software. Now, Microsoft has teams of people working with those companies to prepare them to write applications for the Windows Phone.

Check the Windows Phone Marketplace regularly for new applications.

More Supported Social Networking Sites

One of the attributes that make the Windows Phone unique among smartphones is its integration with social networking sites, like Facebook and MySpace (see Chapter 12).

The next step for Microsoft is to work with even more sites to make adding them on your Windows Phone as easy as entering your user ID and password. When more social networking sites are supported, the Windows Phone will be even more superior to its competition — so you can bet that more supported sites are on the way.

Support for More E-Mail Services

In the future, Microsoft should add more e-mail services to its list of supported sites. Right now, the Windows Phone supports Windows Live, Facebook, and Yahoo! Mail. Look for other e-mail services (like Gmail and AOL) down the road. Then you'll be able to enter your ID and password, and have your e-mail synchronize with your phone.

Although Gmail is managed by Google, which offers the Android platform, it's in the best interest of all companies to cooperate when serving customers.

A Compass

The lack of support for a compass in the Windows Phone isn't well known and bit of a surprise. The lack of a compass means that the Windows Phone can't do things that its competition can do. For example, although the Windows Phone can run mapping applications, it can't do navigation, and specifically augmented reality applications, as well as it could if it had a compass. The Windows Phone can use workarounds to estimate direction, but not as well as it could if it had a compass.

Side-Loading of Music

If you have a CD, its license allows your Zune to play that music just as if you bought it in the Zune Marketplace. Because you may not be able to connect your phone to your PC, you only can get music from the Zune Store, which means that you need to re-purchase the music you already have on a CD (or go without) — neither of which is a very good option. Microsoft should fix this.

Loading of Proprietary Applications

Right now, Microsoft restricts which applications can run on the Windows Phone. Some of the reasons for this are legitimate — for example, it improves the stability of the platform. But it also makes it hard, if not impossible, for companies to write programs for their own employees to use. For example, if a shipping company wants to have an application that allows it to track the delivery of a package, the company can't really do it with a Windows Phone unless it wants everyone — including its competition — to be able to use the application, too. Because applications are only available through the Windows Phone Marketplace, they're available to everyone.

For widespread adoption by businesses, as well as to offer a migration path of any kind for Windows Mobile/Windows Phone Classic users, they need to have a way to add company-specific applications. They can be made available by side-loading or through a private part of the Marketplace.

Connection to External A/V

You can connect your Zune to your TV and your stereo. You can connect your laptop to a large-screen TV or a projector. But you can't do any of these with your Windows Phone. This limitation really keeps the phone from achieving its full capability. It should be done. Microsoft, make it so.

Cut and Paste in Microsoft Office for Mobile

You can type and delete words and images within a Microsoft Office for Mobile application, but you can't cut and paste. Some people within Microsoft have insisted that cut and paste capability aren't important — their argument is that you just use the phone to make minor corrections and customizations.

This may be true, but being able to cut a section of text or an image and paste it into another section is a fundamental capability that most of us are used to using. Not having it undermines the case that the Microsoft Office for Mobile applications are just like what's on your PC.

More Accessories

Yes, cases, headphones, and Bluetooth headsets were out there when the phone first became available. But also look for

- ✔ An A/V docking station to connect your Windows Phone to your stereo and TV

- ✔ External speakers with a docking station so you can play your music

- ✔ A PC synchronization dock, which just looks better than a USB cable does

- ✔ A car connector to offer navigation and connection to your car stereo

- ✔ An external keyboard and full-screen display, like REDFLY (www. celiocorp.com), so you can use a full-size screen and larger keyboard without the heft of a full laptop

Updating of the Operating Systems

If you use a PC, you've probably had the experience of upgrading to a new operating system or a new version of software. In the past, cellphone operating systems were more of a mystery — you never even knew what the operating system was called, let alone that your phone had one. With the Windows Phone, you'll eventually have the option of upgrading your phone's operating system. As with the PC, upgrading will add new features and take care of software bugs.

Index

Apple & Macs

iPad For Dummies
978-0-470-58027-1

iPhone For Dummies,
4th Edition
978-0-470-87870-5

MacBook For Dummies, 3rd
Edition
978-0-470-76918-8

Mac OS X Snow Leopard For
Dummies
978-0-470-43543-4

Business

Bookkeeping For Dummies
978-0-7645-9848-7

Job Interviews
For Dummies,
3rd Edition
978-0-470-17748-8

Resumes For Dummies,
5th Edition
978-0-470-08037-5

Starting an
Online Business
For Dummies,
6th Edition
978-0-470-60210-2

Stock Investing
For Dummies,
3rd Edition
978-0-470-40114-9

Successful
Time Management
For Dummies
978-0-470-29034-7

Computer Hardware

BlackBerry
For Dummies,
4th Edition
978-0-470-60700-8

Computers For Seniors
For Dummies,
2nd Edition
978-0-470-53483-0

PCs For Dummies, Windows
7 Edition
978-0-470-46542-4

Laptops For Dummies,
4th Edition
978-0-470-57829-2

Cooking & Entertaining

Cooking Basics
For Dummies,
3rd Edition
978-0-7645-7206-7

Wine For Dummies,
4th Edition
978-0-470-04579-4

Diet & Nutrition

Dieting For Dummies,
2nd Edition
978-0-7645-4149-0

Nutrition For Dummies,
4th Edition
978-0-471-79868-2

Weight Training
For Dummies,
3rd Edition
978-0-471-76845-6

Digital Photography

Digital SLR Cameras &
Photography For Dummies,
3rd Edition
978-0-470-46606-3

Photoshop Elements 8
For Dummies
978-0-470-52967-6

Gardening

Gardening Basics
For Dummies
978-0-470-03749-2

Organic Gardening
For Dummies,
2nd Edition
978-0-470-43067-5

Green/Sustainable

Raising Chickens
For Dummies
978-0-470-46544-8

Green Cleaning
For Dummies
978-0-470-39106-8

Health

Diabetes For Dummies,
3rd Edition
978-0-470-27086-8

Food Allergies
For Dummies
978-0-470-09584-3

Living Gluten-Free
For Dummies,
2nd Edition
978-0-470-58589-4

Hobbies/General

Chess For Dummies,
2nd Edition
978-0-7645-8404-6

Drawing
Cartoons & Comics
For Dummies
978-0-470-42683-8

Knitting For Dummies,
2nd Edition
978-0-470-28747-7

Organizing
For Dummies
978-0-7645-5300-4

Su Doku For Dummies
978-0-470-01892-7

Home Improvement

Home Maintenance
For Dummies,
2nd Edition
978-0-470-43063-7

Home Theater
For Dummies,
3rd Edition
978-0-470-41189-6

Living the
Country Lifestyle
All-in-One
For Dummies
978-0-470-43061-3

Solar Power Your Home
For Dummies,
2nd Edition
978-0-470-59678-4

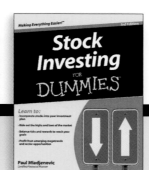

Available wherever books are sold. For more information or to order direct: U.S. customers visit www.dummies.com or call 1-877-762-2974.
U.K. customers visit www.wileyeurope.com or call (0) 1243 843291. Canadian customers visit www.wiley.ca or call 1-800-567-4797.

Internet

Blogging For Dummies,
3rd Edition
978-0-470-61996-4

eBay For Dummies,
6th Edition
978-0-470-49741-8

Facebook For Dummies, 3rd
Edition
978-0-470-87804-0

Web Marketing
For Dummies,
2nd Edition
978-0-470-37181-7

WordPress
For Dummies,
3rd Edition
978-0-470-59274-8

Language & Foreign Language

French For Dummies
978-0-7645-5193-2

Italian Phrases
For Dummies
978-0-7645-7203-6

Spanish For Dummies,
2nd Edition
978-0-470-87855-2

Spanish For Dummies,
Audio Set
978-0-470-09585-0

Math & Science

Algebra I For Dummies,
2nd Edition
978-0-470-55964-2

Biology For Dummies,
2nd Edition
978-0-470-59875-7

Calculus For Dummies
978-0-7645-2498-1

Chemistry For Dummies
978-0-7645-5430-8

Microsoft Office

Excel 2010 For Dummies
978-0-470-48953-6

Office 2010 All-in-One
For Dummies
978-0-470-49748-7

Office 2010 For Dummies,
Book + DVD Bundle
978-0-470-62698-6

Word 2010 For Dummies
978-0-470-48772-3

Music

Guitar For Dummies,
2nd Edition
978-0-7645-9904-0

iPod & iTunes
For Dummies,
8th Edition
978-0-470-87871-2

Piano Exercises
For Dummies
978-0-470-38765-8

Parenting & Education

Parenting For Dummies,
2nd Edition
978-0-7645-5418-6

Type 1 Diabetes
For Dummies
978-0-470-17811-9

Pets

Cats For Dummies,
2nd Edition
978-0-7645-5275-5

Dog Training For Dummies,
3rd Edition
978-0-470-60029-0

Puppies For Dummies,
2nd Edition
978-0-470-03717-1

Religion & Inspiration

The Bible For Dummies
978-0-7645-5296-0

Catholicism For Dummies
978-0-7645-5391-2

Women in the Bible
For Dummies
978-0-7645-8475-6

Self-Help & Relationship

Anger Management
For Dummies
978-0-470-03715-7

Overcoming Anxiety
For Dummies,
2nd Edition
978-0-470-57441-6

Sports

Baseball
For Dummies,
3rd Edition
978-0-7645-7537-2

Basketball
For Dummies,
2nd Edition
978-0-7645-5248-9

Golf For Dummies,
3rd Edition
978-0-471-76871-5

Web Development

Web Design
All-in-One
For Dummies
978-0-470-41796-6

Web Sites
Do-It-Yourself
For Dummies,
2nd Edition
978-0-470-56520-9

Windows 7

Windows 7
For Dummies
978-0-470-49743-2

Windows 7
For Dummies,
Book + DVD Bundle
978-0-470-52398-8

Windows 7 All-in-One
For Dummies
978-0-470-48763-1

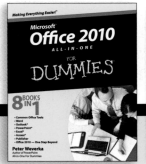
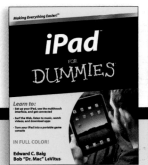
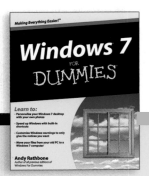

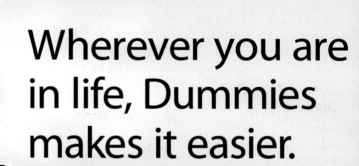

Wherever you are in life, Dummies makes it easier.

From fashion to Facebook®,
wine to Windows®, and everything in between,
Dummies makes it easier.

Visit us at Dummies.com

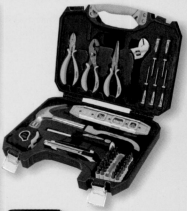